Praises fo.

M000084920

We are most defined by what we overcome. Mike's story is the gritty, inspiring saga of unrelenting tenacity that overcame the longest of odds. It's the story of Rocky—not the boxer— but the one who became a corporate CEO. As is vintage Mike, in its telling, he breathes hope and optimism into us all.

—Robert E. Hall
Former CEO and best-selling business author

Mike tells his story of going from the streets to CEO in a very compelling way. It is filled with pain, frustration, and struggles, with a large dose of compassion. I found it to be a very insightful and encouraging book, and I recommend it to others who are overcoming obstacles on the way to living the life they want to live.

—Renie McClay
Author and Learning Consultant
Inspired Learning LLC

I've just in the past few years connected with my brother Mike (we're half-brothers). As I read Mike's book it was like looking into a mirror! Dysfunctional? Not even close to the life Mike lived. Mike got dealt a very bad deal not of his choosing. Both of us felt trapped with no way out. But we're always *one choice* away from a different life! We all make choices to better our life or bitter our life. I've seen Mike grow into an incredible husband, father, hard working businessman, and a great brother. In Mike's book he gives hope, help, and healing to people who grew up like him. Mike has surrounded himself with incredible people and has become a determined man with a mission to succeed and help others to succeed as well. His book will give people direction and hope for their lives. Mike has taken his mess and made it an incredible message!

This book is a must read for all who have been dealt a tough deal in life. I'm honored to recommend *Rock Bottom*. This book inspired me even more to stay on course and motivate people even more to keep fighting when they feel they're at rock bottom. Mike's book will stir great things inside each reader to keep following your dreams no matter what. Get ready to take a journey with Mike and his heart for *all* to succeed!

—Rev. Ken Freeman
Author of *Rescued by the Cross* and
Toilet Bowl Christianity

Mike's story is powerful. No other word describes it but powerful. It is a story of triumph and success when time and again triumph and success seem impossible. It is a story full of sadness, rich with hope and stuffed with persistence. If you want to get a firsthand look at how someone used hope and persistence to overcome obstacles most of us could only see in a movie, then spend a few hours with this book.

—Jerry Acuff
CEO, Delta Point
Author of *The Relationship Edge in Business*

ROCK BOTTOM

MICHAEL G. COOLEY

FROM
THE STREETS
TO SUCCESS

ROCK
BOTTOM

Tate Publishing & Enterprises

Rock Bottom
Copyright © 2011 by Michael G. Cooley. All rights reserved.

No part of this publication may be reproduced, stored in a retrieval system or transmitted in any way by any means, electronic, mechanical, photocopy, recording or otherwise without the prior permission of the author except as provided by USA copyright law.

The opinions expressed by the author are not necessarily those of Tate Publishing, LLC.

Published by Tate Publishing & Enterprises, LLC
127 E. Trade Center Terrace | Mustang, Oklahoma 73064 USA
1.888.361.9473 | www.tatepublishing.com

Tate Publishing is committed to excellence in the publishing industry. The company reflects the philosophy established by the founders, based on Psalm 68:11,
"The Lord gave the word and great was the company of those who published it."

Book design copyright © 2011 by Tate Publishing, LLC. All rights reserved.
Cover design by Kristen Verser
Interior design by Joel Uber

Published in the United States of America

ISBN: 978-1-61739-738-7
1. Biography & Autobiography; Business
2. Biography & Autobiography; Religious
11.01.04

This book is dedicated to my incredible wife, Lisa,
and two of the greatest kids I know, Sierra and Brayden.

Acknowledgements

This is what I was looking forward to as much as any other part about writing a book. I really appreciate the forum that allows me to thank the people that have meant so much to this book and me. However, to acknowledge all the people who helped me write this book and tell this story would be a book in itself so my apologies in advance if I leave anyone out. At the same time, this book would have never happened if it weren't for the following people.

To my wife, Lisa, who has been my constant supporter throughout my writing of this book. To my children, Sierra and Brayden, it is through them that I was able to realize what it is like to be a kid again.

I had some amazing mentors along the way, starting with my father, whose incredible work ethic and reliability was the basis on which I built my career. To Robert Hall, the CEO at ActionSystems, who showed me that servant leadership and genuine compassion for your employees and customers are always the right answers. If my father was the basis for my career, then Robert was the catapult. To my best friend, Chris Bauer, who showed me how to be creative in every facet of my life. To Joan Faubion, who was the first to give me a public forum to tell my story and make my life relevant. To my brothers, Ken, Marty, and Lionel, all of them completely different individuals but all of them helped to develop me when no one else was there. To all the people that I have worked with and continue to know at ActionSystems, ChartOne, and Quinlan. Every one of these people means so much to who I am today.

To Renie McClay, a renowned business book writer and Louann Swedberg, an outstanding editor who collectively took my scrambled thoughts and memories and helped to make them my life story in print. Finally, to Tate Publishing, whose consultative publishing process put me at ease that I was with the right publisher, beginning with its founder, Dr. Richard Tate.

Table of Contents

Section IV: Mature Adult Years

Introduction

For over seventy-five years, this company has been in business. Three generations of Quinlans have helped to build this business. Now for the first time in its history, the Quinlans have brought in someone from outside the family to take the company forward. Recruited from Dallas, Texas, to Providence, RI, was a big enough move in itself, but when I joined The Quinlan Companies as their CEO in 2006, I would be making a move that took me my whole life to arrive at.

As an adult and as a dad, I started thinking back to my childhood and what advice and guidance I could give my kids on life and growing up. Since I didn't have much parental guidance, I wanted it to be different for my kids. So, I sat down and started writing about my life and all of the experiences I've had. After my family was in bed, I would spend many nights at the computer in the dark recalling incidents and experiences. My purpose? To remember what I experienced and convey it in hopes of helping my kids to understand the life they live and appreciate that the future is theirs to create.

As I kept this journal and wrote my story, I felt compelled to share it with the greater community in hopes that my experiences could reach others and maybe even help them.

Despite a tragic childhood and the deep downward spiral that was my life as a teenager, today I have a wonderful family, and I'm the CEO of a thriving and profitable company. The journey of how I got from there to here has been a long and difficult one, but it has also had tremendous rewards and joy. My single hope is that by reading this story you or someone you know will be inspired and helped along life's journey. I want to encourage you to give it (your life) your all, because your all is truly enough.

SECTION 1:
CHILDHOOD YEARS

Chapter One:

In the Beginning

Even though I was born in the early '60s, my life growing up was not easy. My life was in no way like an episode from *Leave it to Beaver*. I didn't have June and Ward for parents—mine were more like a quiet yet proud dad who marries Mommy Dearest.

Life As I Knew It

I was about four when Dad left. That's when my clear memories start. I was thrown out of toddler land and became very aware of the tornado that would become my life's new reality. The three of us—me, my half-sister Donna (Mom's daughter from her first marriage), and Mom moved into a makeshift apartment in a suburb of St. Louis. What was once someone's garage was the first house I remember as a child. It had a bedroom, kitchen, and bathroom all in one space. The cramped and rundown place was dreary and just barely habitable. Our financial situation wasn't good, and this was the best Mom could find with short notice and short funds. We didn't have much in the way of clothes, possessions, or food. When Mom worked at a bar not far away, Donna and I were alone and had to stay inside. We made do with whatever we could find for food or toys to amuse ourselves in this dismal "home."

It wasn't always that way. Mom and Dad started out carefree and were fun-loving. Before they were married, they loved to go out and often took driving trips to see the sights. It was the early sixties—times were safe, wholesome, and good in our country. Dad had a good job and was making decent money. Mom was a waitress at a bar. Things were going well. They were living the American dream and decided to get married. Shortly after they did, the dream started to crumble. Each brought "baggage" to this relationship built on partying and having fun. Mom had two kids from a previous marriage. Dad's first wife had died. By adding their own two children (me and my younger brother, Marty) the stress was building. The true colors of their personalities came out. Life wasn't as rosy as they thought it would be.

Both of my parents had weaknesses. My mother's was whiskey. Although my dad also had many periods of drunkenness, my mother steadily increased her drinking in the early years. She gained her independence from the bottle and took on a new personality when she was drinking. The more she drank, the stronger she felt. The stronger she felt, the meaner she got. It was a vicious cycle in every way. Dad was sharply aware of the pattern, but didn't do much to stop it. He tolerated it. As he saw the drinking and behavior get worse, he didn't know what to do; besides, he loved his wife. *Alcohol wasn't my dad's weakness; his weakness was my mother.*

The drinking binges were constant as was the drain on the family finances and the frustrations because of it. Tensions were high. My parents always fought and argued loudly. My mom's continued drinking helped her to temporarily soothe the tension (she got so loaded she was often sleeping it off). Her frequent drinking escapades would sometimes go on for days. Dad would be left with house chores, kids to manage and feed and his job to go to. There were four of us at the time: me, my younger brother, Marty, Donna, and Ken. (Ken and Donna were my half brother and half-sister from my mother's previous marriage.)

One of the final straws came in 1966. Dad had worked many long overtime hours to save up $300 for Christmas presents for the kids. Mom gladly took the money and disappeared without a trace. Three days later, she returned in a sports car with a strange man at the wheel. As my dad walked up to the convertible, he found that they were both completely and utterly drunk. Mom was unable to sit up, and the guy had his hand on her leg. Seething with rage, my dad pulled Mom from the car and carried her through the snow and into the house.

All of the money for presents was gone. My mom was sleeping off her alcoholic binge. On Christmas Eve, Dad took what little cash he could scrape up and went shopping to try to salvage the holiday for us. It was a cold and somber holiday. I remember the feeling in our house. Even being a young child, I could sense the tension and pain always hovering just a fraction below the surface. One false move by any of us, and things would explode.

Eventually the booze, tension, and fighting took its toll. My dad lost his job, my parents separated, and Dad left St. Louis. In this breakup, my sister, Donna, and I stayed with my mom in Missouri, and my brothers, Ken and Marty, went with Dad to Texas.

While Donna and I were holed up in the sparse garage apartment, Mom was working at the bar down the street. Sometimes when she came home, we would have dinner. Most of the time, she would just get ready and go out to the bars for the night. We didn't have many sit-down meals, and often there wasn't much to eat. I recall one particular supper when we sat down at the kitchen table (it looked like an ironing board that folded out of the wall). Our entire meal consisted of a pint of coleslaw from Kentucky Fried Chicken—no chicken, just the coleslaw for the three of us. I felt hungry a lot, but hey, it kept me skinny.

In those early days, we spent quite a bit of time by ourselves or with babysitters because Mom was either working or going out. Most times, we would go to the babysitter's house because it was bigger and nicer than our place. My first experience with a sitter started on the wrong foot—literally! I opened the basement door into darkness so black that I could barely see my hands in front of me. I took the first step and reached for the railing, only to discover there wasn't one. I fell over the side of the stairs into the black hole below. Fortunately a metal bucket cushioned my fall before I hit the concrete floor. I landed on my head and ended up with at least a dozen stitches.

Another time, a different babysitter was watching a group of kids. We were playing games on a back porch somewhere. One of the games included going under a table with a blanket pulled over the top. Each kid took a turn hiding underneath the table with the sitter. That's where she taught us a new game —"You show me yours, and I'll show you mine." You can guess what that was all about. I was five or six years old and was being fondled under this table by a sixth grade babysitter. I was mortified—unable to move or speak. Then I felt confused and embarrassed by the new "game." Even though I was very young, something told me that this was not right. One by one as the kids emerged from under the table, each was silent and introverted. The laughter and smiles had subsided. No one made eye contact; no one talked or interacted in any way. When that day was finally over, I was still very hurt and confused by the incident, but I decided not to tell mom about it. She had been very crabby lately and gone most of the time. I was afraid of what she would say or do to me. Besides, I didn't think she would believe me.

Corporeal "Care" in Corpus

After about two years of barely getting by in our dismal digs, my mother's financial situation got even more desperate. She couldn't afford to keep two children *and* support her drinking habit. Something had to give, and it wasn't the booze. To maintain her constant supply of whiskey and nights at the bar, one of her children had to go. I don't remember much fuss about the decision—it was cut and dry. Donna stayed with mom. I was sent to live with my dad in Corpus Christi, Texas.

Being in Texas was the first time I really remember being around my brother, Marty. It was the beginning of a brotherhood relationship that would be the only thing that would keep us sane for years to come.

Corpus Christi was a whole lot different from St. Louis. It was always hot there. The ocean replaced the Mississippi River, and palm trees replaced the buildings of downtown St. Louis. Mom and her constant drinking were replaced with my dad's new wife, Peggy. Peggy had two children, Kenneth and David, from her previous failed marriage. They were several years older than I was. To add to the Corpus Christi collection of family members, my half brother, Ken (mom's son from a previous marriage) was also living with us. Shortly after I arrived, my dad and Peggy had their first child, Lionel. That made six boys, ranging in ages from newborn to teenager, in a hot, cramped house. I thought the St. Louis apartment was bad. This was worse.

From the first day I met her, and for many brutal years to come, Peggy struck unbridled fear in my heart. The picture of her is so clearly etched in my mind that it will never fade. The horror and cruelty exuded by her evil presence was so strong that it literally took my breath away—I instinctively sucked in air in unbridled fear of this being. Physically, she was a huge woman who weighed more than 260 pounds and stood just over five feet tall. Peggy had coarse, wiry, brownish red hair—like a brillo pad. Her daily attire was a dirty polyester housedress without sleeves. Peggy never wore pants or anything other than those dresses. The overpowering smell of her body odor and dirty clothes moved with her. She was always sweating and eating something—the remnants of both would remain on her clothes for days. If her mouth wasn't busy eating (and she ate *a lot*), it was permanently fixed in a menacing scowl. In her watery eyes, you could see and feel the deep pools of the hatred and jealousy she showed everyone. During each instant we breathed in her house, she remained constantly pissed off at my brother and me—always looking for a reason to erupt into a tirade.

Corpus Christi always seemed steamy and unbearable. Living was slow-paced because of the heat. Kids would play outside most of the time. We were no different. It was too hot inside because there wasn't any air conditioning—besides, Peggy was in there. Her presence always made things feel hotter and tense, like a pressure cooker ready to explode.

One afternoon, Marty and I were playing outside. For some reason (I'm sure it was for some unforgivable act like breathing), Peggy stormed out of the house in a full rage. As she came after us, she tore a thick branch from one of her huge rose bushes. She roughly grabbed each of us by an arm and dragged us to the side of the house—out of view. She took turns hitting us on the bare legs with the jagged branch. With each brutal blow, the thorns would catch and rip open our young skin. After a few lashes, I couldn't bear it any longer and screamed out in terror and pain. Her words were savage as she said, "If you don't stop screaming, it's going to get worse!" And it did, as she continued with renewed anger. She continued the whipping until the welts swelled and the blood ran in small streams down our legs. Even though the pain was excruciating, her fierce words had reduced our crying to whimpering and sniffling for fear of worse punishment. To this day, I can feel the sting of the thorns and the pain they caused as they raked through my skin.

At home, pain was a daily event. It was delivered in either physical or emotional abuse heaped on Marty and me by Peggy. The unprovoked beatings and abuse always happened when my dad was at work. For the life of me, I couldn't understand why we were being scolded, ridiculed, belittled, spanked, slapped, and beaten for doing the very same things my stepbrothers and newest half brother did. Every day, Marty and I were terrified of doing something that would set Peggy off. When that happened, she moved from verbal abuse to physical punishment. We were alone in our misery. We couldn't tell Dad what was happening for fear of what Peggy would do when she found out. By the time my dad came home from work, we all behaved well out of raw fear. To my dad, it must have appeared Peggy had done a great job managing a household of boys.

Not too long after I arrived, I watched my half-brother Ken run out of the house and down the street. As I saw his body fade into the sun, I could feel an aching in my heart. Even at such a young age, I knew something very wrong had happened. At seventeen, Ken had run away. He had had enough. I was too young to know my half-brother that well, but I felt that he was the only one who cared for me and Marty. I didn't want him to leave us behind, but he just couldn't take it anymore. He escaped a terror that would be my life for many years to come. As Ken would later write in his book, *Rescued by the Cross*, he had previously endured years of abuse from living with our biological mother and her husbands and boyfriends. Living with Dad and Peggy was another scene of abuse and fear. Ken had already seen this movie, and he was old enough to break away.

Growing up, Dad was a hardworking laborer who always gave an honest day's work. Despite his commitment and hard work in his job, Dad was very seldom recognized as a leader, so promotions were few and far between. Even though he worked all the time, we still didn't have enough money or anything to show for his grueling work or all of the overtime he put in. Our house was a run-down shamble of a thing. It once had white wooden siding, which had long since faded into a dirty gray color with paint peeling all around it. The porch was old with broken boards and steps. The yard was loaded with broken-down pieces of equipment and old junk. We had a gravel driveway with patches of grass and dirt for a front lawn. Nothing grew except for those wretched, thorny rose-bushes. Even Mother Nature was afraid to be too close to Peggy. The garage was a falling down pile of lumber surrounded by more junk in the yard. Since we were two blocks from the segregated part of town, I am sure we were considered "white trash," and our house sure lived up to the name.

Dad was not appreciated at work or at home. At home, Peggy was like a heavy anchor constantly wrapped around his neck. She continuously put him down and called him names. Each time he was excited about an idea to get us out of our financial nightmare, Peggy would immediately make him feel that there was no way on this earth that he could possibly make anything happen. In her words, "That's just another one of your stupid, hare-brained ideas!" To Peggy, he was always an "idiot" or other even worse things. Either to his face or behind his back to the kids, Peggy would chastise my dad. She seemed to hate her own life so much that she took it out on anyone who was within her reach.

Peggy and dad would often fight, yell, and scream about these ideas—and other things— for a few days. That's when we would hide in fear of Peggy's bad mood and the new torture tactics that irritability would help her dream up. In the end, Dad was defeated and never did anything with his aspirations. Being a loyal person, he was forced to live his life in the shadow of someone who would never support him or his dreams.

Dad wasn't a real nurturing or demonstrative person. I cannot recall a single time that he told my brother or me that he loved us. He did try to show his affection in his actions as best he could. When he was home and had the energy, he made a real effort to divide his time between us five boys.

It was during this time that I first witnessed the devastating effects of drugs on a person. Kenneth, my stepbrother (Peggy's son) was thirteen years old, and he had been making some money by mowing lawns. No one really noticed that he spent a lot of time out back in what was the garage until the day we discovered him passed out on the ground. We couldn't wake him up. Dad and Peggy thought he was drunk. As we tried to pick him up, the gas fumes hit us. Kenneth had been sniffing gasoline for a cheap high. Apparently, he had been doing it for many days, and he was near death. As we rushed him to the hospital, his heavy and lifeless body lay across our laps in the backseat of the car. I watched his eyes roll back into his head, his breathing seemed to stop, and I thought for sure he was dead. The long, frightening drive to the hospital seemed to take forever, but finally we got Kenneth there. He eventually got better, but I don't know if he ever fully recovered.

School as a Sanctuary

It was in Corpus Christi that I started school. I liked going because I found sanctuary there from my hell at home. In the first grade, I went the whole year and never missed a day of school. As a reward for perfect attendance, my teacher gave me a silver dollar. I have never forgotten that first reward or how proud I felt getting it. It is one of the positive memories I have from childhood.

During the day, school was my only escape and it's where I first came in contact with kids—and girls of my own age. I had my first crush on a girl who looked just like Cleopatra to me. Her black hair was cut in a very chic bowl-shaped design. During recess, I walked right up and kissed her. This innocent act of love got me my first paddling in school. The second one came in the second grade where I once again got in trouble with a girl. This time it was for pulling her ponytails. No one bothered to ask me why I did it—it was just like at home. Without question, I was guilty and was punished. (If someone would have asked, I would have told them that I pulled her hair because she'd been kicking me in the shins all morning.) I was confused about the opposite sex and how to act. The kids would tease me for whatever came into their minds but sometimes I would help it along, like the time I was once again the new kid in school and I wore a pair of pants that I had ripped the crotch out of night before. I was afraid that I would be in trouble if Peggy found out that I had ripped them at home, so I thought I could go to school and say it happened there. The kids had a field day with me. School was not turning out to be a sanctuary for me anymore.

Summers in St. Louie

During the summers, we were sent back to live with my mom in St. Louis. We looked forward to these visits to escape the constant torment of our step mom. Besides being very jealous of my mom, Peggy wanted to make sure we didn't share any of the abuse details with her. She made it clear before we left what would happen if we told Mom. Sheer terror kept Marty and me quiet. We could relax and not worry about physical abuse—we just had to worry about Mom's drinking and the consequences it brought. Eventually, the summer would end and returning to my stepmother would always have its painful consequences.

One summer, shortly before going to St. Louis, Peggy found another reason to punish my brother and me. She grabbed us and threw us on a bed. Neither one of us had shirts on (we spent a lot of time without shirts or shoes in Texas, because it was always scorching hot). Peggy flogged us brutally with an old leather belt all across our backs. During the whipping, Marty and I looked at each other trying not to cry. (Over time, we had learned how to deal with the pain and control our tears. Tears and cries of pain only made Peggy more irate and brutal.) As I looked at my brother, I recall the hopelessness and emptiness in his young eyes. He looked at me pleadingly wanting to escape this hell. That look still haunts me to this day.

Shortly after that beating, we went to Mom's. While we were changing our shirts, she noticed the unhealed welts. We stopped in our tracks and held our breath for fear of what would come next. She went absolutely ballistic. She screamed and threw a fit. Then she got on the phone with Peggy and my dad. In her tirade across the wires, Mom vowed to come down and kill Peggy. (I heard later that Peggy was afraid for her life.) Marty and I were cowering in the next room, not knowing what to think. We prayed that we didn't make things worse for when we returned, and a small part of us hoped against hope that maybe this would make the abuse stop. Mom had found out and maybe things would be better.

Other than the threatening phone call, my mom didn't do anything else to stop the violence she knew was happening. My dad on the other hand did do something—he left Peggy. The separation was short-lived, though. He returned, telling us that he didn't want Lionel to come from a broken home like we did.

Eventually, Mom wasn't immune to hitting us either. When she would get drunk (which was daily), she would release her tensions and frustration with her life on us. Mostly, she would yell and scream. We were frightened, but it was more tolerable than the beatings. However, one day that changed. She burst into my room as I was looking through old comic books. She slapped me in the face and accused me of things that I couldn't even understand at the ripe old age of nine, much less have participated in. This came as a huge shock and a devastating blow. I thought that at least with my mom, I was safe from the physical abuse. From that point on, unprovoked "discipline" in the form of physical or mental abuse was constant, no matter where we were.

Each year when Marty and I returned to St. Louis, my mother was in a different efficiency apartment. She was frequently evicted for not paying her rent or for making excessive noise when she was drunk. The apartments typically had one main room that made up our bedroom and living room. There was a small kitchen and a bathroom. Most of the places were not more than 400 square feet in size.

Just like when we were little, during the day my mom would go to work as a waitress. Marty and I would be cooped up in the small space by ourselves. My sister would spend most of her time elsewhere—usually with boyfriends. Mom told us that we couldn't go outside. Only later would I realize it was because she didn't want anyone to find out that we were being left alone. She was afraid that they would call the Child Protective Services on her for leaving eight- and nine-year-old children alone.

For the most part, we were pretty good kids (of course, I am biased) and we kept busy watching our old twelve-inch black & white TV or making sandwiches with every ingredient we could find in the refrigerator (which wasn't very much). The sandwiches never tasted very good, and our stomachs growled a lot. We didn't complain because we were just happy to have reprieve from the hitting and yelling.

One day, as brothers do, my brother and I got on each other's last nerve and began to fight. We had seen it all and had learned from the best. Out of nowhere, I came upon a chain and hit my brother across the back. He went into a fit of rage and grabbed a huge ceramic ashtray. He crashed it over my head knocking me out. I was on the kitchen table out cold. When I came to, I could hear my brother on the phone to our mother. In a panicked voice he was screaming, "I killed him! I killed Mike!"

"You S.O.B.!" I said to Marty as I came to.

"Mom, Mike's not dead. I got to go!" Marty quickly hung up the phone, ran into the bathroom and locked the door. He stayed there for the entire afternoon until Mom got home and rescued him from my fury.

Mom was rarely at home for very long before she would change her clothes, freshen up, and be on her way to the local tavern. Often she would leave us alone at night too. Many nights we would hear the sounds of yelling, gunshots, sirens, and fights going on right outside our window. Other times we would be dragged with her to the local drinking establishments.

I will never forget the smell of the bars and the people. The places were dimly lit and filthy so the drunks could hide in the darkness hoping to avoid the shame that had become their lives. My mom was right there with them.

There were bars on every corner, and we knew them all. Some opened at 6:00 a.m. Marty and I spent many summer days there from early in the morning until late in the evening. We were the local drunks' favorite kids. We would hustle them for Cokes, a meal, and juke box money. I still can hear the sound of "Take It to the Limit" by the Eagles playing in the background of my mom's favorite bar, coincidentally called The Limits. It was at these places that we met many of my mom's boyfriends. A lot of these guys' names would appear on the "list" on a chalkboard near the entrance of each bar. Having your name on the "list" meant you were banned from the bar for a reason like fighting, being drunk and disorderly, or having bad credit. Some of these guys would become our future stepdads.

Texas Tormenters

Back in Texas, in the third grade it was discovered that I had a speech impediment. (No, I don't mean my southern accent.) This impediment involved a lisp. I just couldn't seem to say anything with an "s" in it. My dad had me work with a speech teacher, but my lisp got even worse, so they pulled me from the class after only a few weeks. This turned out to be another reason for kids to make fun of me. Add the lisp to the flat top haircut, discount polyester pants, checkered shirt and one pair of shoes a year, you had a kid that could give the other students infinite reasons to tease and pick on me. My brother and I were constantly teased at school. If the ridicule wasn't occurring at home by my stepmother and stepbrothers then it was happening at school. Needless to say, my self-esteem and confidence was low and I felt constantly beaten down. Was I a bad kid that deserved this treatment? What did I do wrong? I couldn't figure it out. Marty was the only other living being who understood what my life was like. We didn't talk about it much; we knew it was us against the world.

Marty and I continued to be harassed by our stepbrothers. When Peggy let up, they would take over. It was endless. When my dad was away, we never knew what tormenting or abuse would happen. That year, my dad and Peggy were in a bowling league and left Kenneth and David in charge of us. This was like giving an addict free dope. Our stepbrothers would perk up when the bowlers were on their way. They worked hard to maximize their time tormenting us. One example was when Marty and David were fighting over a can of dog food to feed the dog. My brother was trying to open it with a can opener. David lost his temper because it was taking too long.

David was meaner, bigger, and older than we were, and was just as savage as Peggy.

He grabbed Marty's hand, stuck it in the can opener, and began turning the handle. As the blade cut into Marty's flesh, he let out a scream. I jumped up and ran to his rescue but it was too late—the damage was already done. David realized that there was tangible evidence of his tortuous ways. He threatened that we'd better tell our dad that it was an accident if we knew what was good for us. After being beaten down so many times, our will was gone. We didn't tell what really happened. Marty ended up with a long scar that has never faded. This would just be one of the many scars we would collect over the years. This one was a deep physical scar, but the mental ones cut even deeper.

Kenneth and David were more brutal to us than any two kids could be. But to make it even more confusing, they also considered us their property. One day, I was walking home from school with some of my classmates. I had some packets of mustard in my pocket and wanted to show off. I put the packets on the sidewalk and jumped on them to make them explode all over. What can I say? It didn't take much to impress young kids. As I jumped on the second one, everyone let out a gasp. I saw the fear in their eyes as they gaped at the horror behind me. I slowly turned to find that the mustard had exploded all over the pants of the school bully; just my luck.

Fights are like honey—sticky messes that always seem to attract all kinds of creatures and vermin. Suddenly, all of the kids nearby flocked to see me get killed. The bully looked down at me and in a deep voice said, "Lick it off."

I was frozen in place with fear. He grabbed me pushed me down on knees and said again, "Lick it off."

I was afraid of him but it wasn't the same gripping feeling of terror that Peggy struck in me. No way was I going to do this. As I was bracing for another beating, I heard a voice say, "Lick it off yourself." I looked up to see Kenneth. He told me to get up and go on home.

As I walked away, he stood face to face with my enemy. The bully backed down and left.

Then there was the time that we were away from home. All of the kids had to sleep in one bed. As I was trying to sleep in the hot and stuffy room, I felt a hand touching me inappropriately. Before the shock of that really sunk in, the same someone was trying to get on top of me. I was wide awake now and freaked out. I threatened to wake everyone up if he didn't leave me alone. By the grace of God, he stopped. Needless to say, I was incredibly traumatized. The horrible act kept playing over and over in my head. I couldn't sleep at all that night or for many to come. I began to dread nighttime and darkness for fear of similar incidents. It took many agonizing nights and days to put that trauma behind me.

The first ten years of my life were spent bouncing back and forth from one place to another. I must have lived in fifteen different places during the first decade of my life. I was constantly being shuttled back and forth from Mom's to Dad's, depending on the season of the year and who had the resources to feed me. Daily abuse and torment at home and school were a way of life. Marty and I lived in constant state of fear and uncertainty. We didn't have many things or much food. All we had was fear and each other.

Chapter Two:

My Tale of Two Cities

By now, it was the early '70s. Times were a bit freer—not as conservative as the previous decade. Both of my parents moved around a lot. While my dad moved all over the state of Texas, my mother wasn't so brave. She stayed near St. Louis. Because we moved so much, my brother and I never had much of an opportunity to make friends. Any budding friendships during the school year were cut off when we went for the summers in St. Louis.

There was one summer; neither one of my parents could afford to send us back to Texas for the school year, so we started school in St. Louis. My dad had lost his job, and if my mom had any extra money, it went down her throat. When we got back to Texas, my dad was still between jobs, so we stayed with Peggy's parents. The rotten apple didn't fall far from the tree— this was a rough scene. Peggy's dad was a sheriff in a small Texas town. He always talked about "niggers" and how he had been running them out of town. But when Marty and I started school in St. Louis, right before we moved back down to Texas, we went to an all black school. Very confusing times indeed. This gave Grandpa more ammunition to run down blacks. I didn't see color as a distinguishing trait of people. I only saw acceptance or rejection. Even in this school, Marty and I were tormented by the kids. Thankfully, it wasn't long before Dad got a job and we moved out.

We were living in a trailer park on the outskirts of Burleson, Texas. (Yes, the home of Kelly Clarkson.) My dad didn't drink much anymore but occasionally his life got to him, so he'd throw a few back. One such night, Peggy and my dad had been drinking. From there, one of the thousands of arguments they had started. This particular argument became so heated that my dad bolted from the trailer, taking my brother and me in his drunken flight to nowhere. It was late at night, and Dad was driving while completely smashed out of his mind. Marty and I were terrified as we bounced around in the back seat. The car flew at high speeds over a dark and dangerous dirt road. Dad was furious to begin with and exploded in a renewed rage when I asked him to slow down. He responded by slamming on the breaks. As the car skidded to a sudden stop, Dad turned his bloodshot eyes to me and screamed, "If you don't like the way I'm driving, then get out!"

After the third time he yelled, "Get out," I did.

As the car squealed away, the dust and dirt kicked up into my face. I watched as the tail lights disappeared leaving me in complete darkness. I was alone, with nothing in sight and only the clothes on my back. (There were no cell phones in those days. Even if there were, we wouldn't have had enough money to even think about getting one.) There I was, in the middle of nowhere in a night filled with sounds of the wild. It was frightening. I was trying to be strong and decide what to do when I saw some faint lights approaching. Dad backed up the car and Marty let me back in. The fear in Marty's voice commanded me to be quiet. My lips trembled as I clenched my teeth to help me keep my mouth shut. It was a long and dangerous ride back to the dismal trailer park, but we kept quiet.

Gainful Employment in Gainesville

Not long after, we moved out of the trailer park to the booming metropolis of Gainesville, Texas, a town of about 12,000 people. Dad took a new job. I was getting bigger and wanted a bike. Dad said I would have to earn it. So at the ripe young age of eleven, I got my first job as a dishwasher in a truck stop on the outskirts of town. I was tall for my age but short for fifteen (which is how old I told the manager I was so I could get the job). They hired me at $1 per hour, or $8 a day. The job was grueling, and it didn't last long—just long enough to pay for my bike and start my hunger for working.

I worked various jobs on weekends and after school. I did everything from throwing newspapers to washing dishes in various diners. My dad, raising five boys and feeding a stepmom that could out eat all of us combined, couldn't exactly afford much of an allowance, so I was on my own. It was hard work, but I wasn't really good in school and I liked making money. Having my own money gave me a sense of accomplishment and hope.

Again, the school year would end and we would be back to St. Louis with my mom. My sister was now in her late teens and in many relationships. She eventually ended up dating Larry, who was an African-American. For the most part he was a nice guy—he turned me on to Motown, including Marvin Gaye. Occasionally their arguments would turn violent. One night Larry grabbed Donna, threw her against the wall, and started choking her. I watched in disbelief as he lifted her off the floor by her throat. As she gasped for air, all eighty pounds of me jumped on Larry's back and grabbed him around the neck. I hung on for dear life, beating him with my fists and screaming for him to stop. He flung me to the side then realized what he was doing. I was bruised and sore, but at least I stopped the violence. He broke down and started to cry.

My mom despised Donna's relationships, especially those with minorities, but did her best to tolerate it. Meanwhile, Mom had her own issues with relationships. Nothing slowed down her dating and partying; I couldn't possibly count the number of men my mom brought through the door of our cramped one-bedroom apartment. They would have to step over Marty and me as they crept to the bedroom. The living room floor is where we would sleep. We spent many a night pretending we didn't notice these loud and clumsy "guests" who stepped on us and smelled of the bars. Meeting men, barhopping, and drinking was a way of life for Mom. If she wasn't drinking at the bars because she had spent her money, she was at home with a glass of water and a bottle of whiskey making life miserable.

Left to Our Own Devices on the Streets

When Mom was home, she was more than happy to let us go out on the streets. We made friends wherever we could find them. Most of the kids we met had a dysfunctional home life like we did, and their parents didn't care if they roamed the streets either. Even back then, the streets were rough and dangerous. We started to blend in with the rest of the crowd. We started picking up their habits and vices. We didn't let the fact that we had no money stop us from getting something if we really wanted it. This eventually led to stealing. We started small by stealing candy from the neighborhood store then moved on to clothes and shoes. It was a habit that was hard to break.

Sometimes we got caught stealing, but because we were so young they assumed we didn't know any better. We knew exactly what we were doing. Two of my first partners in crime were twins who were also growing up in a rough home life. They used to get very afraid and edgy when their dad started drinking. There were many nights that we would sit outside and listen to the parents argue. Sometimes we'd hear the fights escalate into physical confrontations. That's when the twins, not even teenagers yet, would rush in and try to protect their mom. At that point, my brother and I would head home, trying not to hear the screaming and slamming sounds that filled the dark night air behind us. We knew them ourselves, only too well. The next day, the twins would have little to say but the many bruises on their bodies spoke volumes about what happened.

It was with these twins that we found more friends through a hole in a fence that led to a scrap yard in a warehouse. This place was stocked with retail store rejects and out of date products. It was a kid's treasure trove of slightly damaged stereos, toys, and candy.

Like ants crawling over discarded food, we rummaged through the mounds of trash for several days. We carried off the treasures we found. One day as we were digging through the stuff, there were sirens all around us. Like roaches when the lights come on, more than a dozen kids from ten to fifteen years ran in every direction. There wasn't time to make it through the fence, so I tried to hide in the piles of junk. I was surprised when I heard the sound of gunshots. As I looked through the rubble, I saw the neighborhood legend, Cocoa. Like something out of a B-rated cop movie, Cocoa was a skinny, slick-haired white guy who carried a gun and a badge. Just as he ran by the fence shooting into the woods at the kids, he stopped dead in his tracks. He turned to aim his mirrored sunglasses and gun right at me. "Don't move," he commanded.

The police rounded up about ten kids and put us into a line against the fence. After giving us a stern warning, we were released. I guess you can say we dodged a bullet, literally. Even though I had seen the cops close up at my house, it was usually because my mom was in a domestic dispute with a lover or she and my sister were fighting and a neighbor called for help. This was the first time that I was involved with the police. I was lucky that day, but it wouldn't be the last time the cops would be looking for me.

As kids, we were always going on little missions—adventure and escape was always the goal. We used to hop freight trains and ride them across the city until the railroad people shot rock salt from their shotguns at us, and we'd be forced to jump from the moving train. Sometimes we would jump off the trains into Hobo Jungle. The stories were rampant about how the hobos would kill any kids that came there. In fact, there were two kids that had recently come up missing just before we entered hobo haven. There, we found shacks of cardboard and wood made by homeless and criminal types. Most of the structures were clearly temporary, but a few were very elaborate. One was complete with rooms, furniture, food, and toiletry items.

As we were exploring this new world, we heard a noise in the trees. The grunting sound suddenly grew louder and turned into yelling. We took off away from the hut into the trees, running for our lives. The hobo was irate and was ready to kill us with his bare hands. The adrenaline pumping through our young bodies from the terror helped us outrun him. We were lucky that night—we escaped unharmed. It was so frightening that we would never return.

Then summer ended, and we were back at my dad's in Gainesville. It would be the first time I would go to the same school for two consecutive years.

Searching for Salvation

Sometime during those childhood years, my half-brother, Ken, got back in touch with us. We went to San Antonio to visit him. By then, he had married and was on his way to building a successful career as an evangelist minister and a singer. I can remember how we looked up to Ken—we thought he was so cool. He had escaped the reign of terror and abuse we were still living, and he was successful! He would sing in coffee shops, he had an album out, he drove a cool old car, and we thought his wife's parents were rich. He was definitely a charismatic and passionate preacher. He made quite an impression on us. We had a slight glimmer of hope that we could also find a way out of our lives of terror and despair.

My brother and I were about nine and ten when we went to hear Ken speak at his church. Ken took his profession very seriously and coached us before the service to behave ourselves. Unfortunately, we didn't have any type of religious upbringing, so we were clueless about what was going on or how to act. We were also kids with a lot of energy who got bored easily. We did pretty well until the last hymn. During one part of the song, everyone raised their hands to the heavens while singing and rejoicing, including us. However, since we didn't know the words to the song, we struggled to keep the songbooks in our hands as we raised them to the heavens. The books wobbled and nearly fell on our faces a few times, but we concentrated on the words as we sang and tried to hold the songbooks high in the air.

Because we were sitting in the back of the church, only Ken could see what we were doing. Right at the climax of the song, Ken, at the front of the church, busted out laughing in front of the entire congregation. Everyone stopped and stared as Ken continued to laugh. Our wide eyes and fearful looks as Ken laughed and the people looked at us, betrayed the truth that we hadn't a clue about what we were doing or that it was such a funny sight. We finally realized that no one else was holding their books in the air. We put our arms down and were as quiet as church mice after that.

It was during that trip with Ken that Marty and I were saved and accepted Jesus Christ as our Lord and Savior. Together, we knelt down beside a bed and prayed together. Even though we were young, it was a very moving and lasting experience. It would be several years before we would see Ken again.

Over time, I did manage to make a friend or two. I met many kids that were lost like me. I was beginning to realize that I wasn't the only one having a tough time at home. One of those friends was Joe. While Ken was the first one who tried to turn me on to Jesus, I had many other Jesus supporters along the way, including Joe. He invited me out to his church on Wednesdays and Sundays. Life at home was so unbearable that I would do anything to get away, including going to church. Joe's way of practicing religion was even more confusing to me than Ken's. Joe used the excuse of going to church so he could see a girl he was dating. It took at least forty-five minutes for us to get to the church by bus, and half of the trip was on a dirt road. We stepped off the bus in front of a shotgun house with a steeple on it. The hand-painted sign out front read "Church of Christ." I remember thinking, "I rode all that way for *this*?"

Joe would ride out every Sunday morning, go to mass, and stay with this girl, Rhonda, then come back to church Sunday evening. At the conclusion of Sunday evening services, he would take the bus home.

While Joe was dealing with poverty as bad as my own, Rhonda had to deal with a rape at age thirteen. She would relive the horror of this violent act every single day when she saw her attacker—her father. As a result, Rhonda was so confused about sex and needed so badly to be needed that she thought sex was what she had to do to be loved. I soon understood why Joe stayed all day at Rhonda's.

Eventually Joe broke up with Rhonda and guess who started dating her? Yours truly. The devil and his temptations were everywhere, and I was too blind to see them. My previous history of being fondled by a babysitter and nearly raped by a family member also caused me to be confused about sex and love. Rhonda and I didn't last long, though. Her neediness nearly suffocated me, but we remained friends and we never had sex.

Religion would also follow me in St. Louis. The twin brothers who were also living a life of physical abuse at the hands of their father were also lost and searching. Marty and I went to different churches with them as well. It's almost ironic. I don't think I can recall either of my parents going to church, yet my brother and I had been to more churches than most people I know: Church of the Nazarene, Catholic, Methodist, Pentecostal, Church of Christ, Baptist, Jehovah's Witness, and Nondenominational, just to name a few. I guess at my tender young age, you could call me a connoisseur of churches.

While we would never admit it, during these childhood years Marty and I were looking anywhere and everywhere for someone or something to throw us a lifeline and save us from our hell on earth. We were poor, abused, and afraid. We had no confidence, no positive role models, and no hope for change. Although we had been "saved" when we were with Ken, we needed something solid and good to hold on to—to get us thru our insane existence. We were young, inexperienced, and alone. The adults and kids in our lives tormented us constantly. We didn't have anything or anyone, other than each other. We didn't know what to look for or how to get out of the deep, dark, and dangerous holes that were our lives.

Looking Back

I still recall the wonderment of being a kid and how even the simplest of events in my childhood would make me feel happy inside. I also recall how the emotional and physical abuse is etched in my mind. I often wonder if I had stayed in one home, with one set of parents, going to the same school district, how I would have been different. Still, I am proud of where I have come from, and I honestly believe I am a better person for enduring what I endured.

Today, I am trying so hard with my own kids to give them a stable life with two parents that love them very much. Even though you will read that they too had some different homes, we stick together as a family.

Oh, how I look back on my childhood as a great learning experience and I look to my kids as my second chance to live a different childhood through their eyes and with their hearts. Through them, I feel born again and I never want to take them for granted.

I also learn from people like my mom and Peggy. I can understand how it must have been hard for Peggy to raise five boys, particularly two of them that were not her own. For my mother, she was never in a long-term relationship, and it was tough to make ends meet by herself. Then there was my mom's struggle with alcohol. I can now at least appreciate the internal struggles they both had to endure.

SECTION II: TEENAGE YEARS

Chapter 3:

Teenage Rebel

Many say, "The bigger the kids get, the bigger their problems are."
I know this is true—I lived it.

The teenage years are when all the fun begins. Kids start to grow up and begin to become more like adults—both mentally and physically. Mentally, teenagers can understand, reason, see logical connections, think abstractly, and begin to predict outcomes of actions. Physically, their bodies are like racecar engines burning calories that cause them to grow by leaps and bounds. The growth also fuels the racing hormones and recognition of the opposite sex. Kids begin to develop tastes and preferences in music and ways of life. They begin to form relationships with others that shape the core of their beings and guide the direction of their lives. Teenagers continually strike out into the new world of adulthood and often revert back to the familiar world of childhood.

It was in 1974 in Gainesville, Texas, that I remember noticing my appearance. Lots of the teenagers you'd see on TV or in magazines wore their hair long and wore bell-bottom pants with wide belts. I was going on thirteen and what looked back at me from the mirror that day wasn't much. I hardly recognized myself anymore. I was a tall, scrawny kid with basic, brown hair buzzed into a flat top. My wardrobe included very few low-budget clothes from the local

K-Mart. Because we didn't have very much money, I wore those same cheap clothes over and over again until they were in tatters. If I was lucky, I had one pair of shoes that had to last the year. I hardly resembled those teens I saw in the ads.

As you might imagine, with the constant harassment at home and the endless teasing at school, I was an insecure kid. I was quiet and kept my head down. My physical appearance and the emotions that were bubbling to the surface didn't help either. My self-esteem was in the dumper and I was painfully aware that I didn't fit in anywhere. I never talked much with the kids at school for fear that I would give them some new ammunition to tease me about. I didn't invite anyone to my house because it was an embarrassing, filthy mess (even I could see that). And then there was Peggy.

There were a few rare times toward the end of the school year when it seemed that I was just starting to fit in and make a friend or two. Right about that time, the school year was over, and I would be off to St. Louis for the summer.

Taking a Stand (Then a Run)

At home, Marty and I were getting fed up with the years of abuse and harassment. Half of our young lives had been spent being afraid and tortured. Everywhere we'd turn in the small house, it was there: the yelling, thumping, smacking, hitting, and verbal abuse. We rarely fought back, because we had learned the hard way that the consequences were always far worse. We did whatever it took to be quiet and invisible.

One day it all came to a head with David. He was mad about something and decided to take his frustrations out on me. He was much heavier than I was and had me in a painful wrestling hold. I didn't cry out, but was struggling with all of my might to get out from under the big, hot, sweaty bully. Fortunately for me, it was Marty's turn to take out the trash. When he saw David on top of me, he took the trashcan and hit David upside the head, and the blow knocked his hold loose. Together Marty and I bolted out the door and down the street. We knew better than to return before Dad got home. David would have told Peggy an exaggerated story of what happened, and we knew she'd be waiting to show us how she felt when we messed with her kid. (We weren't her kids by *any* stretch of the imagination. We were nothing but a source of constant irritation and an outlet for all of the misery and hatred she felt about her life.)

Marty and I always depended on each other because we were all we had. From early on, it had been us against them. Really, it was us against the world. We had no allies here or in St. Louis. We finally decided that day that we would not tolerate the torture anymore— no matter what the consequences. Our resolve led to other acts of resistance against the stepfamily. We worked together to outwit our assailants every chance we could. We even began to reject our father, blaming him for not doing anything to change our hellish situation. That summer, we pressured Dad big time to let us go live with Mom during the school year. He would not budge. After some months of enduring grief from us and the constant verbal berating from Peggy about how worthless we were and how much it cost to raise us, he finally wore down and gave in. My brother and I got to go to school in the big city.

Moving on a full-time basis to St. Louis became a turning point in our lives.

> Until then, we had been prisoners of small towns and small apartments. We were subjected to years of physical and mental abuse wherever we were. We felt like caged animals living in fear of our surroundings.

In St. Louis, now that we were older, Mom could go to work then go out and party. She could leave us alone without being worried that she'd be sent to jail because we were too young to be left alone. It was like suddenly being freed from a lifetime in a cage and released into a huge new world. We were elated. There was a small glimmer of hope that life would get better for us. What we didn't know was that this new world would be a jungle of wild, hungry animals waiting to feed on fresh, naive meat.

Our first year was harmless enough, Marty went to sixth grade at an elementary school and I went to seventh at the junior high. As always, we definitely stood out in our schools—we dressed differently and poorly; we had funny haircuts. Our southern accents combined with a country upbringing and poor manners caused us to be laughing stocks and butts of many jokes. Kids can be so cruel. School wasn't much fun at all. Home was worse. We were living in another small efficiency. Donna was always with her boyfriends or going out. Mom was working during the day and partying the night away. Marty and I were on our own to make it the four miles to and from school every day. We scrounged up what food we could find in the apartment and survived on that and the funded lunch programs, which gave us a meal at school. At least we weren't being physically tormented. We made it through the year and went back to my dad's for the summer.

During that following summer back in Texas, my brother and I reached the boiling point with our stepfamily. Things there had not changed at all. It was still hot, dirty, and degrading. Peggy, still as enormous and mean as ever, tried to maintain her mental stranglehold. She constantly told us how worthless we were and that we'd never amount to anything. The other boys were the same also. My half brother, Lionel, was as spoiled as ever and seemed to relish in getting us in trouble. Our stepbrothers kept the physical pressure on by hitting, thumping, tripping, or mouthing off to us every time we passed by. Knowing that nothing we could tell Dad would change the situation, Marty and I were again left to fend for ourselves in the foul and disgusting rooms of our small house where we baked in the stifling Texas heat.

We would escape the abuse and decay by going outside or hanging out with friends. I also spent a lot of time at the Boys Club—I would do anything to avoid having to go home. However, sooner or later, we would have to go there.

The house in Gainesville had two bedrooms, one bathroom, a kitchen, dining room, and living room. So with my dad, Peggy, four brothers, and me, the house had to be retrofitted to accommodate our family. Marty and I ended up in the dining room, which became our bedroom. That room was right in the middle of the small house. Everyone walked through it to get to the kitchen or the bathroom. Privacy and peace were out of the question.

In addition to the house being so small for six people, it was full of stuff, and was dirty and hot! There was no air conditioning in our house, so hot was an understatement. There were piles of dirty clothes, papers, boxes, books, knick-knacks, old broken-down appliances, car parts, just junk everywhere. When the house got full, things would be tossed on the old back porch, in the yard, or in the falling down garage. Dirty dishes were consistently on display in the kitchen. Half-eaten food and leftovers were littered among the dishes; spilled, sticky things coated the faded, torn linoleum, and the constant aroma was the strong smell of old leftover food. The flies and roaches seemed to like it. The kitchen was a war zone: humans against insects. We were constantly swatting flies and luring the roaches into traps. It didn't seem to bother Peggy, either. She was always in there eating something, and she had us on assignment to clean up after the mess was created. Needless to say, we were never really good at it. There was no dishwasher—well that is unless you consider Marty and me; technically all the kids were supposed to assist with the chores, but it always seemed that Marty and I were the ones tricked or bribed into doing it by our stepbrothers. Some of my first memories of that kitchen were standing on a crate washing the dishes by hand.

It was in that kitchen of this house that the reign of physical abuse would end.

I was standing in there being screamed at by Peggy for the millionth time in the seven years I had known her. I had probably finished the last of the milk. Her tirade went on and on. When her large body paused for some needed air to continue the ranting, I responded with a disinterested remark. That did nothing but set her off with renewed fury. I reacted quickly as I saw her uncovered and sweaty, massive tree trunk of an arm swing into my face. With both hands and all of my might, I caught her wrist. Then with every ounce of energy I had, boosted with years of pent up rage and disgust, I slammed it down to the counter and yelled, "No! It ends now! No more!"

With those words, I stormed from the house. I had made up my mind in that instant that I would never take abuse from her or anyone else ever again! I went far away from that place and my tormenter. That night, Dad came home to a more irate than usual Peggy. She had been waiting all afternoon to give him an earful. She told him that I refused to let her hit me. I remember being nearby and hearing Dad's reply.

He said, "What did you expect?" As he walked away, Peggy became even more enraged and continued her rant with a new ferocity. I could be wrong, but I like to think Dad smiled ever so slightly as he walked away from the wicked woman spewing endless hate from her mouth.

Hormones, Horror, and Hopelessness

That was just the beginning of the teenage changes, challenges, pressures, and learning. It was during this summer that I went to visit my brother Ken for about three weeks. I stayed with him, his wife, and his small baby boys in San Antonio. Ken was really making a difference and doing something with his life. He was preaching and singing in a large church and was also working very hard at a bank downtown. He worked the late shift in an early version of a computer room.

One night, I went with him to work. After a while, I left the bank and walked a few blocks to an arcade to kill some time. After running out of what little money I had, I started walking back to the bank. It was pretty late at night by then. In the dark, an older car pulled up beside me. The driver, a man, about thirty years old, rolled down the window and asked if I wanted to get high. I was bored, didn't have any money, and I knew what getting high was, but I'd never done it before. Intrigued by the offer, I said, "Sure, I got a few minutes." *What the hell*, I thought.

We went for a ride, smoked a joint, and carried on a conversation. This guy was a gym teacher at the local junior high. As he talked, we drove further from the city. After about half an hour or so, I told him that it was about time for me to head back to meet my brother. He looked at me and hesitated, then began his story. He told me about his girlfriend and her kinky vices. He offered to pay me to be with her so he could watch us. I could tell that this idea got him excited. In my naïve and high state, I thought it could be interesting—I needed money and hey, I'd like to find out what it's like to be with an older woman. So again I thought, *what the hell*, and said sure.

We continued driving on dark roads to reach his house in the suburbs. When we got there, I was still high and getting a bit drowsy. He showed me to the bedroom and said he was going to get his girlfriend. I was seated on the bed, still feeling no pain, getting sleepy, hungry, and was vaguely wondering what this would be like. A few minutes later, the guy came back and told me that she wasn't home but was on her way. He sat down on the soft bed in the darkened room beside me. Together we waited, not saying too much.

After a few minutes of not talking, there was an awkward feeling in the air. The tension seemed to be building, or was I just getting paranoid from the pot? The lights dimmed as we waited for the girlfriend. I was drifting off to sleep. The guy shifted closer to me on the bed. That movement put me on high alert. Now I was paying attention. The room was suddenly small, very dark and very warm. I began to get sweaty and confused. I felt a hand reach out to touch and slowly rub my leg. At that moment, the fog cleared and the horror of the situation fully registered in my young mind. I jumped up and freaked out. I started waving my arms around, pacing and babbling about how I wasn't into this type of thing. I was trying to be forceful and convince both of us that this was wrong. Without looking at his face, I continued to pace and told him that he better take me back immediately. As he sat there in the dark not responding, I became more agitated. He finally got nervous, and we left.

It was a long and tense ride back. Every moment that we inched closer to the lights of the city, I began to feel better physically, but my mind was still racing. What had just happened? How the hell did I get in this situation? What would have happened if I had gone along with this situation? My adrenaline and emotions were still rushing. This wasn't the first and it wouldn't be the last time that my sexuality would be compromised, leaving me with a million questions and emotions battling in my head.

When I walked back to the bank, Ken was livid when he couldn't find me. He went off about how long I was gone and how I was supposed to have been back by a certain time. I was still in shock from the experience but managed to make up a story about where I had been. I was too embarrassed and humiliated to tell what had really happened in that dark room. As he went on yelling at me, I thought about how stupid I was and how things could have gone very differently with that man. Given the alternatives, I guess I was glad to have Ken yelling at me.

During those times, sex and my sexuality were confusing to me. My hormones were always raging, and there was a constant nagging in my mind and body. Back at Ken's, I had a Playboy magazine that I would enjoy with my vivid imagination in the bathroom. One day while lost in lust, I heard Ken's wife knock on the door. I panicked and hid the magazine under the rug. As I walked out, I could see the obvious lump where I left it. I was busted. Later that afternoon, Ken and Debbie confronted me about it. Once again, Ken was extremely upset with me. He wasn't prepared to deal with a situation like this. I'll never forget his line of questioning. He asked me if I was showing the book to his sons (they were seven and eight). Of course I wasn't. The thought that he would think such a thing made me question what kind of person I was. Then I wondered what he really thought about me. That question came up again in my mind after his occasional criticism for not being more athletic—never exercising or playing sports. I was a young, isolated, and abused teen who needed support and understanding from someone somewhere. In my mind, I thought of all the places I could get support; it would be with my brother, the preacher. Man was I disappointed.

Any small glimmer of hope I had for help and a way out began to die and was replaced with deep despair.

It was time to go back to Gainesville.

Messin' with Marty

That fall, in St. Louis, I started the eighth grade. Even though this was junior high, it was full of kids that were using it as a waiting room for dropping out of high school. The school was full of drugs, gangs, and pimps from the roughest part of town. These so-called "kids" were tough and like me, most had a very tough upbringing.

Marty and I still stuck out and were loners. That made us easy prey. A few days into school, Marty was walking the few miles home and as always, he passed by the corner store. It was an old building where the school tough guys hung out and made their drug deals. There was a wall outside the store where they would wait for their prey and harass vulnerable passersby. Behind the store was an alley that was a good hideaway for conducting drug deals or just doing drugs. The guys grabbed Marty and pulled him into the alley where they started taunting and scaring him. When they were bored with that, they started punching. They beat him just for being different and because he was in the wrong place at the wrong time.

By the time Marty got home, he was crying and humiliated. Both my mom and I were incensed beyond reason. Vengeance was the only thing that would quench our fury. All three of us got in

Mom's convertible and began the hunt. Marty saw one of the bullies, Jack, walking down the street with his followers.

Before the car stopped, I had already jumped out. Jack knew what I was there for, so he dropped his books and got ready. He had no idea that there were many years of pent up anger and frustration just waiting to explode, and it was going to erupt all over him. With all my might, I lunged into Jack and I slammed him into a wall. Jack was a good fighter, but he was no match for my fury on this day. I could hear his friends cheering him on, trying to will him to a victory. I was tired of a lifetime of teasing, being picked on, and being abused and mistreated. I was even more fed up with it happening to my brother. My fury was so fierce that every time Jack would swing, I had already hit him three or four times. I had him down on the ground, pounding him in the head over and over again. I slammed his head against the concrete. Somewhere on the edges of my consciousness, I could faintly hear him pleading, "Okay, I give, I give!"

But I didn't—I couldn't. My rage had not even begun to be released. I grabbed Jack and was ready to launch him through a store window when finally a familiar voice broke the spell. I heard my mom yell, "Mike, stop! I don't want to pay for the window!"

In that instant, I knew I had to stop. We couldn't afford the window or the trouble from the police. I pushed him away. His face was battered and bloody. By then, the cheering for Jack had stopped was replaced with silence and looks of shock. I stared long and hard into the eyes of each one of the kids standing there, the rage still burning. I turned to my family and walked away. The punks got my message loud and clear.

Back at the apartment, Donna was with her boyfriend, Larry, and one of his friends. Larry's friend wasn't your average looking guy. He was about six-foot-seven and weighed about 250 pounds. When my sister heard the story, she was also infuriated. This time, my mom and brother stayed home and Larry, his friend, and I went to look for one of the other perpetrators, Billy. Our first stop was the corner store, and we pulled up just down the street from the store. While I walked over to the wall, Larry and his friend went into the store. There were four or five guys and a few girls leaning up against the wall, but no Billy. I went up and said, "Where's Billy?" The looks I got said "Who the hell are you, country boy?" I walked up to two of the guys and I said again in a fiercer voice, almost yelling, "Where's Billy?" At that moment, two guys on either side of me started closing in.

As I was surrounded by four guys ready to pummel me, a huge black hand came flying over our heads and landed against the wall. The shadow of Larry's friend alone backed the guys away. He asked in a very deep and menacing voice, "Where's Billy?" All four started spilling every piece of information they could about Billy's whereabouts. They must have warned him, because we never found Billy that evening. We went home drained and tired, but somewhat satisfied. My brother and I knew that our lives at school would be different from here on out. That was okay by us. The old way sucked anyway. We could take whatever they could dish out (or so we hoped).

The next day, Marty and I met at lunch and eventually had to go out to the field like everyone did after lunch. The field was behind the school. It had concrete bleachers that lined the entire back portion of the school. At the bottom of the bleachers was a track that circled a field. Everyone hung out on the bleachers or on the field until lunch period was over.

As Marty and I headed toward the field, we saw Jack, Billy, and the rest of the toughest bunch of losers you would ever meet. They saw the two scrawny Cooley boys in our usual garb of cheap clothes. From the field, they started to make their way up the bleachers and straight for us. I told Marty to stay close, and I pushed him slightly behind me to my right side. As they reached the top of the bleachers, my heart was pounding. I was no longer filled with the anger and hatred that drove me to attack Jack the day before. I didn't feel tough anymore. The truth was that I was scared beyond belief, but I would not let them see my fear. So, I stood as tall and as firm as I could while they surrounded us.

Jack walked straight up to me. He lifted his hand toward me, and I backed up. I was ready for whatever was going to come next. I had taken many beatings before, what was one more? I could handle the physical side, but emotionally I knew if I didn't stand up to these guys, the scars would run deep, and we'd continue to be tormented for the rest of our time there. I was dreading that prolonged agony.

Then the most amazing thing happened. Jack reached out to shake my hand. As we shook hands, he apologized for messing with my brother. He also said, "You sure have a good punch." I was stunned and speechless. Then Jack turned to Marty and shook his hand. After a moment of introductions, they turned and walked back down the bleachers. We'd survived.

Fitting In—In All The Wrong Places

After that, things seemed to change for us. My brother and I were beginning to fit in. We started hanging out with all kinds of people now, from tough guys to nerds, from stoners to jocks, both black and white alike. We thought we were making good friends. My brother started to hang with Jack and his friends on a regular basis, and I started hanging with some guys that were a little older and got into a little more trouble.

We were now with the "in" crowd. We started wearing worn-out jeans and growing our hair long. Then we began doing what was at the time, in the mid-'70s, the ultimate thing to do to fit in—drugs! We didn't start out slow. In eighth grade, I was doing everything there was—smoking dope, popping Quaaludes, Valium, Speed, Acid; you name it, and we tried it.

School became an afterthought and a nuisance. It was so easy to skip school on a regular basis. Donna would pretend she was my mom and call the junior high and get us out of class. The guys we hung out with thought we were really cool because we could skip school. They would skip too and hang out at our apartment. Donna would buy us beer and cigarettes, and sometimes we would be so drunk before Mom got home, we would have to leave and come back after we sobered up.

One day I skipped school to hang out with a couple of guys that were a few years older than me. They had already dropped out. We spent the whole day and into the evening smoking dope and drinking. When our partying reached a peak, someone suggested that we break into something. This suggestion set off an evening of crime that would be talked about for a long time.

By the time the morning came, we had broken into an elementary school, a newspaper office, and my very own junior high. We trashed the rooms and broke into offices to steal money and steal things to sell. The next day when we divided our spoils, it was a couple hundred dollars each. Two of the guys put their money together and bought a car. What did I do with my earnings? Me and another guy spent the day at a pinball place where we played games all day and night. (Hey, I was fourteen, you know?)

When I went back to school days later, everyone was still talking about it. When we were roaming the empty halls a few nights earlier, destroying property, vandalizing, and urinating all over the walls, we didn't think of how many people it would affect.

A few days had passed, and I was actually starting to believe I had gotten away with this despicable act. During the final exam in history, the classroom was silent and everyone was focusing on the test. Breaking the silence, the teacher called my name. Naturally everyone looked up. There at the door were three detectives and a police officer. As I approached them, they escorted me to the principal's office. It turns out that my so-called "friends" gave me up.

I was taken to the detention center where I spent eight long days awaiting my trial. In detention, I learned that only the strong survive. The ordeal began with the high-pressure wash they gave me when I was processed. The water and the humiliation also did a good job washing away any dignity I might have had. The other guys in the cell taught me what it took to survive in there.

Since it was my first offense, I was finally released on my own recognizance. Eventually, I went to court and again, since it was my first arrest, I was given a year of probation. The other guys involved were a little older, but they basically got off with a slap on the wrist, allowing us a new chance to commit more crimes.

> I was fourteen, still skinny, doing drugs, partying, and skipping school. Now I was the one picking on people. My attitude had changed. I was acting cocky and invincible. I started stealing not because I needed to, just because I thought I could get away with it.

The drugs, alcohol, partying, skipping school, and now the arrest convinced my mom that I was out of control and was too much for her to handle during her sober moments. She sent me back to my dad's in Gainesville. I was back to being the human ping-pong ball again. Whenever things got tough, they batted me back and forth.

My dad probably thought he could get me in line, but he didn't understand that I was in the middle of a full-blown rebellion and a teenage meltdown. I trusted no one; I thought I was tough and that nothing could touch me anymore. Hope had been replaced with despair, and I had a hardened heart and spirit. Underneath the surface, the emotions, anger, and frustration were swirling out of control. I did my best to keep the years of torment under wraps. Not having a stable home or adult role models was taking a big toll. The hormones, emotions, drugs, and drinking did nothing but turn up the heat under this caldron of toxic emotion. Straightening me out wouldn't be an easy or quick process for anyone.

Chapter 4:

High School, Small Town USA

Going back to Texas and starting at Gainesville High was really different. It's ironic how when I moved to St. Louis and started junior high, I was definitely the outsider with my short hair and funny clothes. Now, a few years later, I'm back in Gainesville and I'm still the outsider. In St. Louis, it was cool to have long hair and wear old ripped up clothes, but this look wasn't popular around the cowboys and jocks of Gainesville in 1976. Once again, I was a minority, an island of one. There was still my friend Joe, who was now a cowboy and excellent athlete. Joe welcomed me back, but I wasn't much into the kind of things he was, so we only hung out occasionally. I ended up behind the school with the cigarette and dope smokers.

Lessons in Futility

During my school years, I had good teachers and bad teachers. One of the bad ones was the athletic coach. One day I got into a fight in gym class with one of his star basketball players. He broke us up, grabbed me, and pulled me to the side. I attempted to plead my case, but he didn't care to listen. In front of the entire class, he started pushing me and telling me to "Go ahead, go ahead take a swing." He said, "Cooley, you know why I pick on you? Because I don't like you, and you're more my size." (I was taller than he was, but I wasn't

140 pounds soaking wet). After a few minutes of humiliating me in front of the class, when I didn't react, he stopped pushing me and dismissed me with the rest of the kids. He didn't know that I was very familiar with humiliation, and it was something that I had become accustomed to.

On the other hand, one of the classes I did enjoy was art. In fact, I was even pretty good at it, and became a teacher's aide for the year. One of my drawings won a school award and was displayed in a glass case in front of the principal's office. The drawing was of Jesus Christ kneeling in a garden before a rock praying. A ray of light was shining down from the heavens across his body. Funny that I would choose to draw something religious for art. You'd never see that today in a high school, which I think is really very sad.

While there wasn't as much trouble to get into in Gainesville, I still managed to stay in trouble. My stepmom was finding my dope, my grades were bad, I was fighting with my stepbrothers, or I was having trouble with girls. The usual story there was that the girl's parents would hate the fact that their daughter was dating a long-haired troublemaker. So, even though I had a number of different girlfriends, the relationships didn't last very long.

Once I dated the daughter of a truck driver. To say he wasn't too crazy about me would be an understatement. We used to have to sneak around to date. When she was dog watching one day, she invited me over. I hopped on my motorcycle and made my way over there. Someone must have been watching the house because after a few minutes, we heard a pickup truck screech to a halt outside. She yelled, "Quick, it's my dad! Go out the back door!" I panicked and ran toward the back door. Before I could turn the handle, the door flung open. Her dad rushed in and started punching me in the face. Then he threw me out into the backyard, followed by some choice words and threats. Shaken, and all of fifteen, I got on my motorcycle and left.

A Business Lesson

A bit later that year, I got a job as a roofer. The job entailed mopping hot tar over a 20,000-square-foot building, in a 110-degree Texas summer. The tar was so hot and sticky that if it landed on your skin, when you pulled it off, a layer of your skin came off with it. I know this from painful experience. Some days were easier—I only had to carry 75-pound packages of shingles up a shaky ladder to the roofers. It was a brutal and extremely physical job—but it was a *job*! I didn't mind doing the work because I was away from home, being productive, and earning money. This gave me a sense of accomplishment and worth. Because of that, no matter what they asked me to do, I always gave it my all.

During my roofing career, I befriended an older guy who told incredible stories of all that he had done in his life. It was the first time an adult took an interest in me (excluding that athletic coach down in San Antonio). I was captivated by this worldly traveler who was now making his living as a roofer. I started to pick him up and give him a ride to work. (Yes, I was fifteen years old and had a car.) My car was a 1969 Chrysler New Yorker with a 440 HP engine. I loved that car! To me, that vehicle meant more than just transportation or a place to fit seven or eight girls at one time. It meant freedom, independence; something of my own; an escape from my hell at home; a place to sleep. Even though my experiences had hardened me, I was still able to meet people and open up to them. I could feel their needs and try to help them out. My new friend needed a car more than I did, and he offered to buy it for $650.

Six hundred and fifty dollars was a good deal and big money for me. Not only would I get money for the car (when he got his first paycheck), but I would also be getting my first paycheck after working in that hellhole job for a month. As a part of a good faith agreement, he gave me $100 and said he would pick me up for work the next day, payday. He never showed up. What could have happened? Dad gave me a ride to work that day. As we drove up to the office, (which was an empty dirt field with a small trailer house for the office), it looked suspiciously deserted. Sure enough, the place was empty and there wasn't a soul in sight. This outfit went from small town to small town picking up jobs, hiring unsuspecting workers only to take the money from their customers, not finish the job and not pay the local employees they hired. Then they would "fold up shop" and run, except this time they also got a car in the deal. The car I had worked so hard for was gone; as was the adult I befriended and trusted. This was definitely one of my more valuable learning experiences.

Texas Jams

That same year, I went to my first big rock concert. I will never forget the Texas Jam. I convinced my dad to drive me and a buddy, Larry, to the Cotton Bowl in Dallas. It was an event that started at 11:00 a.m. and ended at 3:00 a.m. the next morning. The amazing lineup included some relatively new bands like Van Halen, Bon Jovi, Heart, Ted Nugent, Aerosmith, and the veteran band Mahogany Rush. The stadium was packed with teens and young adults.

In those fourteen hours of heat and music, I experienced the biggest party on the planet. There were drugs, alcohol, naked bodies, and sex everywhere, the whole time. No one cared who you were with. Everything and everyone was shared. My emotions and hormones raged. I felt a constant frenzied high at that concert. One wave of passion and emotion was replaced with the next one coming. All of my passions—sex, drugs, rock and roll (and alcohol) were there in excess. My body and mind were ripped open, and I took it all in hungrily.

When it ended the next morning, Larry and I were exhausted, still drunk, and had no clue how we were going to get back to Gainesville. We forgot to figure that part out ahead of time. As the still-buzzed crowd was filing out, we met a couple of older girls that had a car. Fortunately we "influenced" them to give us a ride back home. That ride was a blur. I was exhilarated, spent, and sick all at the same time. When we had arrived at the Cotton Bowl, we were fully clothed but when we got home, all we had was a pair of ripped up jeans. We lost our shoes and the shirts off our backs…literally!

Larry and his brother Robert were interesting characters. Their father was in the military, so they had traveled all over. When they landed in Gainesville, their dad was done with the military and was driving a truck. They were pretty popular with the drug-induced high schoolers and did well with the girls. While Robert experimented with drugs, he never really took to them. Larry, on the other hand, became enthralled with the drug scene. Eventually, he started dealing, and his popularity grew within the drug-using community. My brother and I hung out with both of them. I hung out more with Robert and Marty more with Larry. We became kind of popular and had girls too, but we were hanging with the wrong crowd. The drugs in our lives started to take control.

> When I realized that I would never be able to maintain a relationship with popular girls, I settled for dating girls whose lives were as upside down as mine.

One such girl was Sandy. She came from a single-parent home and eventually was kicked out and lived with her grandmother. One night, she was also kicked out of her grandmother's house. She came over and we were hanging out in front of my run-down, paint-peeling house. I had recently got my driver's permit, so we were sitting on some old car I had just bought. It fit in perfectly with our house. We were on the hood of the car making out while trying to figure out where she was going to stay. My dad, looking out the dirty windows with all of his high morals, came out of the house called me to the side. He told me to stop making out in front of the house, take Sandy home, then get right back!

We got into the car and drove off, but we didn't have a clue as to where we were going. Eventually, we ended up at the local carhop restaurant that was on the drag. There, we met up with some of my hoodlum friends and hung out on our cars. Suddenly, my dad's car whipped into the parking lot and came to a sudden stop. He jumped out and started yelling at me and grabbing me by the arm. One of the guys I hung out with, Bob, was about six-foot-six and about 240 pounds. He didn't know what was going on, so he walked up to my dad and asked, "You got a problem?"

The question set off all six foot, 160 pounds of my dad and he turned to Bob, got right into his face and said, "Yeah, I got a problem. This is my son, and I'm taking him home. Now, *you* got a problem with that?"

Bob backed off and meekly said, "No sir, I'm sorry." So Dad had humiliated me in front of my friends and my girlfriend. I had to go with him, leaving my car and my girlfriend in the parking lot. Another car and all that hard work gone! On the way home, Dad said that it was time for me to leave. I was furious with him for what he had done. So I packed what few things I had and hitchhiked the nearly 650 miles back to St. Louis. That long, hot, lonely walk gave me plenty of time to think about my life as a ping pong ball going between my mom's and dad's. The cauldron of rage and emotion was stirred and boiling over.

Chapter 5:

The Rage

Webster defines "rage" as the following:

[1]rage; Function: noun
1. a: violent and uncontrolled anger
   b: a fit of violent wrath
   c: archaic : INSANITY

2. : violent action (as of wind or sea)

3. : an intense feeling : PASSION

I would have to agree.

I arrived in St. Louis with nothing but a heart filled with anger to a mom who was completely out of control. She was partying all the time and would come home drunk. Sometimes she didn't want my brother (who also returned to St. Louis via a more normal mode of transportation) and me to be there, so she would start a fight then call the police to take us out of the apartment. Welcome back to life with an alcoholic!

Streets of St. Louis

I started to spend a lot of time on the streets and at other people's houses. Sometimes I would have no one to stay with, so I would stay outside. When it was cold, I would find a blacktop roof over some of the local shops or apartment flats. There, I could sleep next to the chimneys that would block the wind kept me from freezing. Other times, I would just duck into an alley and huddle up in a doorway to get out of the wind. There, alone, I'd wait for the morning to come, praying for a better day than the day I just lived through. I was homeless, with only the clothes on my back and a few bucks in my pocket. Many times Marty was also on own his own—coming and going from Mom's place.

I hooked back up with those "good friends" that had turned me in for the destruction spree a few years earlier. When my two buddies learned I didn't have a place to stay, they were more than anxious to help me. They let me in on the fact that that they were getting an apartment, and I could be the third roommate. All I needed was my portion of first and last month's rent. Even though I didn't have quite enough money, somehow all that I had was acceptable. They took it gladly. Finally, I was going to have a place to call my own. I put what few belongings I had with me into the one-bedroom apartment. I went to get the rest of my small stash of stuff from my mom's. When I got back to the apartment, it was *empty*. Gone were my money, my belongings and my "buddies." I was cleaned out again. When would I ever learn?

The bad news: I was out all the money and most everything else I had. That left me with the clothes on my back and the worn boots on my feet. The good news: the landlord didn't know me, so he couldn't come after me for next month's rent. I stayed a couple of nights and hit the streets again.

Sooner or later, I would go by the apartment when my mom was sober, and she would want me to come and stay with her. My relationship with Mom was always strained and unpredictable. Sometimes I would stay for a while, and then I'd be back on the streets. There were many nights when I would be staying at Mom's that I would receive a late night call. Like clockwork it would be Mom, completely sloshed without any money to take a cab. I'd have to walk to the bars, try to find her, and maybe I would have enough money for the cab. If not, I would walk her home.

One night, I received the call and it was my mom in her usual condition. She was calling from the pay phone at the bar. She told me to get to the bar right now. She was, "Getting ready to kill somebody!"

I said I was on my way. I wasn't too concerned because I had seen this *sooo* many times. As I hung up the phone, I could hear my mom screaming at someone, "You guys have had it now! My son is coming up here to kick your butt!" I got dressed and made the walk to the bar.

I'm sure the whole time these guys were wondering what type of psycho son she had. Once I arrived, the skinny, scrawny sixteen-year-old kid, I stood there looking up at two huge guys. After the laughter subsided, I did my best to apologize for my mom and gathered her things. Humiliation was my ally during these late night rescues from the bars. Without it, I'm sure I would have been beaten senseless many times by these drunken deviants. As always, I escorted her out as she continued yelling obscenities back at the bar. *It was painfully obvious; my mom was the town drunk, and we were the laughing stock of the neighborhood. Rage and embarrassment seethed under my skin and kept me warm during the long, cold walks back to the efficiency apartment.*

Finding a New Family

I'd had it with my family, all of them—the heavy, overbearing, abusive ones in Texas, and my out of control, alcoholic mom in St. Louis. I decided to start fresh. My new family consisted of a group of teenagers. I spent most of my time with them. There were about seven guys and five girls who were regulars. We always had other people that would be hanging out with us, and occasionally we would let someone else join our group. It wasn't until later I would realize this family was the equivalent of a street gang.

We were from the south side of St. Louis and started to build a reputation for trouble, fighting, and drugs. Mike and John were two brothers that would party with us until late at night, and like clockwork, they would get up and leave the party. We wouldn't hear from them until the next day. Billy, who loved to drink, was sixteen and was well on his way to being an alcoholic. He seemed to be drunk every day. Bobby was the funny man of the bunch and was always willing to try the latest drug. Eddie was Italian and was a little fireplug of misguided energy. Buzz was half African American and half American Indian. He did his best to distance himself from his heritage. Then there was me. For the most part, I was the arbitrator. While everyone else was ready to fight at the drop of the hat, I was the one who would try to bring reason to the situation. Most of the time, I wasn't very successful.

The girls in the gang were just as cocky as the guys and would fight in a heartbeat. The basement where two of the girls lived basically became our hangout. We would party there all the time, drinking, doing drugs, and passing the girls around. We couldn't remember who was dating who from one week to the next. Sometimes their parents would try to tell us to be quiet or try to make us leave before we were ready. One of the girls would tell them where to go or Billy would get a little upset and get in their faces, and they'd quickly back down. They were afraid of us and didn't know what we might do to them.

Seeing Red

I met a girl outside of the gang named Diane. I thought I was totally, completely in love. She was fifteen years old and already had a son from a previous relationship. Like many girls, she was able to wrap me around her finger. I always wanted to be around her. I should have known she was just too wild. She flirted with my friends all the time. She was always looking for action.

One night, we were out riding around in Buzz's car drinking. Everyone was feeling the alcohol. Buzz and Eddie were in the front, and Diane and I were in the back seat. Diane was getting bored with me and wanted a little excitement, so she pushed away from me and jumped in the front seat between Buzz and Eddie. When she started making out with both of them, I snapped. "Let me out of the car!" I said in a psychotic voice. When he didn't stop immediately, I grabbed Buzz by the shoulder and said, "Let me out, now!"

Buzz let me out in front of my mom's apartment. As I walked up to the plate glass doors of the complex, once again my rage took over. Without even stopping, hands first, I went right through the glass. The door and the surrounding glass came crashing down all around me. I stood there for a moment, and then I turned and started walking. I walked miles with no direction. I began to feel kind of cold during the hot summer night. When I passed under the lights of a 7-11, I realized the damage I had done to myself. Lifting my arms, I could see that both of my hands were red and caked with the blood that was draining from my body. As I continued to stumble forward in the dark, I was feeling cold, numb, dizzy, and weak. Somehow, in a fog, I ended up on the doorsteps of Diane's parents' house. They took one look and rushed me to the emergency room. After what seemed like hours and several blood transfusions, I felt better. The doctor told me that if I had waited much longer, I would have bled to death. He stitched up both arms and I was back on the streets on my own.

One night, not long after the stitches, we were at a party at this girl's house. She was one of those types that were always trying to hang out with the bad boys. The party was something to do, so we went; besides, her parents served some pretty good drugs and alcohol. There were about forty teenagers at the party. Connie was only fifteen, and her parents were in their forties. We got completely blasted. As usual, the party ended with a fight. The fight got out of control. Lamps, tables, pictures, and other personal family items were destroyed. When it finally ended, the house looked like a hurricane came through. The cops arrived and broke everything up, but no one went to jail so we called that a good night.

Is There a "Mike" In The House?

The next day, I went back to Connie's house. While I was there, her dad asked if I was Mike, and I said I was. He asked if I was ready to start working.

I replied, "Sure." The next day, I started working at a grocery store that Connie's dad managed. We wouldn't find out for several days that Connie's dad had me confused with the other Mike that I hung out with. Eventually, Mike got a job there as well, but he lasted less than two weeks. My career at the grocery store would last almost two years.

I really enjoyed my job. It felt good to be appreciated by customers and to be told by my boss and the owners that I was doing a good job. That had never happened to me before. I always worked hard and gave my best efforts. It was here that I got my first promotion. It was the evening before a big holiday sale. I closed out my register and took my drawer upstairs to the management office like I always did. The owner's office was located through a door and up a flight of stairs. It was like an eagle's nest where they could watch over their territory. In their perch, the owners would watch for "bad guys." As I walked through the doors, I could hear them both yelling. One was on the phone, and the other was just yelling at the air. It wasn't long before I realized what the fuss was about. The cleaning crew was not coming in, and the owners were livid. As I handed in my cash receipts, they hardly noticed me. They continued to rant about the impossibility of getting another crew in at such a late hour. As they continued to fume, I left the office and proceeded to the stockroom.

Gil, one of the owners, looked up and said to the other owner, Mike (yep, another Mike), "Would you look at this!" Down below, I had started mopping the floor. I had more than half of the 20,000 sq. ft. store done before they had noticed. It was right then that Gil came down and promoted me to full-time night manager. So when I started my shift that evening, I was a stock boy. By the time I finished, I was a night manager. My hard work paid off that night.

The grocery store gave me an outlet for my evenings. In fact, I was pretty busy all the time. I was going to school during the day, and I got out early on a work release program. I took a bus from out in front of the school to work where I worked from 3:00 p.m. to 11:00 p.m. On the weekends, I also worked another part-time job moving furniture. I never minded the work. *I was addicted to the good vibes I got from doing a good job.* Even with all that time accounted for, I still found time to hang out with the gang and get in trouble. In fact, because I now had money, I suddenly had more "friends" than I knew what to do with. Also with the money came an increased use of drugs and alcohol.

I guess most kids get in trouble from their parents for not going to school. In my world, neither my dad nor my mom supported my education. All of my "friends" had already dropped out. I was out of control in my classes—my grades were bad, and I didn't care about homework or studying, or even going to class. My lunches were spent doing drugs. My teachers were fighting a losing battle trying to teach me anything. In Gainesville, you could take the same elective for four years and each year, you would advance to the next level. Not so when I transferred to St. Louis. This high school would no longer let me take art, which was the driving force for me staying in school. I could only take art as an elective for two years, so I now had to take something else, and I just wasn't the wood shop kind of guy.

School Sucks

Besides me, this whole school was pretty much out of control. Fighting was commonplace. There were fights between races, gangs, and students, and even the teachers were involved. One day, going from class to class, I came across a crowd. I tried to make my way around it. When I got to the front of the commotion, I could not believe my eyes. The crowd was cheering on two brothers who were fighting it out with the principal and assistant principal. I mean they were going toe-to-toe fighting the principals, and the brothers were winning.

My classes were out of control as well. One day, there was a final exam in our math class. There we were, the losers taking a final exam. For several minutes, we just sat staring into space trying to think of ways to cheat. The teacher's patience was wearing thin, and suddenly he burst out, "Anyone who is not going to take this test seriously can get the hell out of my classroom." And with that remark, half the class made like a dart for the door, and I was right with them. What the heck was he expecting? His class was right before lunch, and our entire group of dropout "friends" were waiting for us.

The only thing that had kept me in school, art, was gone. With no support outside of school and no help in school, I did the ultimate—I dropped out. So about three months into the eleventh grade, I dove into my job headfirst and got serious about working on my career in the grocery industry. Looking back, I realize dropping out of school was just one of the many major mistakes I made in my life.

I was doing a good job, and the owners trusted me with everything, including aisles stocked with liquor. Somehow, no matter how bad my addiction to drugs and alcohol got, I couldn't steal from the people that were giving me a chance. I loved the feeling of responsibility and praise—it gave me a different type of high. I was getting addicted to this good feeling of working hard and succeeding.

Eventually, the grocery store fired Connie's dad. As a result, my empowerment and responsibility continued to grow. I was responsible for hiring and firing; I even hired my brother to come to work for me.

The Never-Ending Party

One night, some of Marty's friends came up to work, and he asked if he could take a ten-minute break. Well, ten minutes turned into thirty and then forty-five, so I went to look for my brother. I found him in the basement with his friends sitting on some milk crates in a circle. In the middle was a pile of marijuana roaches. Marty and his four friends had just smoked an entire bag of weed. I sent him home because he was clearly in no condition to work. Eventually, our working relationship came to an end when he continued to call in sick to work. One Friday afternoon when he called in sick, it was the last straw. I could hear a party going on in the background. Marty could barely contain his laughter as he tried to keep up the charade. I told him to go ahead and take the evening off; in fact, take off indefinitely. He didn't seem to mind. I couldn't believe he would blow such a great opportunity!

I didn't have a lot of room to talk because I was still a steady partier. Since I had dropped out of school, I had even more hours to perfect my craft. When the parties were over, there was no telling where I would end up. Sometimes I would go to my mom's, or I would stay at a friend's house, or maybe I'd stay in a vacant house sleeping on the floor. Occasionally, if I was lucky, I would meet some girl and she'd sneak me into her bedroom. I would be able to sleep in an actual bed with clean sheets, but I had to be out before the daylight came. No one wanted to be caught with the likes of me.

There were so many nights that were filled with drugs, drinking, girls, sex, and fights. It seemed the only reason I was working was to support the partying.

> When I think back about all the drugs and alcohol that went through my body, I am certain that I should not be alive.

God had a purpose for me. During these days, the highs were low cost—marijuana, speed, Valium, glue and Rush (like glue, Rush was an inhalant).

The inhalants were some really scary stuff. I could literally watch as it destroyed the brains of people I knew. Which begs the question, why would I try it? I look back, and I still get sick thinking about that time in my life. We were teenage kids sneaking in the dark to the basement window of a house. By sliding a couple of bucks through the window, you'd get your reward. It would be a half of a soft drink can with a liquid product used in making glue that we called Tulio. We would pour the liquid into a rag and then put it into a used bread bag. The open end of the bag would be used to breathe the liquid in and out (huffing). Instantly, you would be incoherent, dizzy to the point of being unable to walk. It was a cheap high that smelled horrible. Night after night, teenagers gathered in darkened corners of schoolyards, alleyways, and parks, huffing. You couldn't huff in enclosed places, because the smell was just too strong. There were dark times throughout my life, but these were truly some of the darkest.

We were destroying our brains and futures, but I still couldn't see what this was doing to me.

Lost on the Tracks of Life

The revelation came one night when I was walking the railroad tracks and found a young girl sitting alone. She looked like she could have been any parent's daughter—she was something special. As I walked up, she reeked of the glue. She was crying, and it looked like she had been crying forever. Through the tears, she shared with me that she had ruined her life and she couldn't stop huffing. She was planning to kill herself. Although she was hallucinating and paranoid, I knew she was serious. She felt her life was over, and she was going to end it. In her, I saw myself and my future. We talked for hours until she forgot about huffing and saw a little hope for stopping. As we sat there in the dark on the tracks, I knew that I was really talking to myself too, and that I was done with huffing forever. She said I was an angel who came to save her. She said she would be okay. She didn't know how wrong she was—she saved me that night, and I was a long way from being an angel.

Out of Control

It was a cold night, New Year's Eve, 1980. We left the safe haven of the gang's territory and crossed into enemy lines. We wanted to go to a party in another part of the city. Most of the parties got crazy. This one was no exception.

The party was in an old house—it was big and dark in there. There were lots of people and noise. There was music somewhere, with many conversations and fights breaking out all over the place that no one seemed to pay attention to. The drinks came fast and often, which was a good thing. We wanted to party hard. Everyone there did too. That desperate feeling was thick and like a dark kind of fog that you could feel in your bones. The layer of smoke in the room was just like the drunkenness that was clouding my mind and dulling my senses. After a couple of hours, we were smashed out of our minds.

We were so loaded that everything was surreal and dangerous. When we were playing darts, one guy was pulling his darts from the board, and another, without looking or paying attention, threw his dart at the board. The dart hit the back of the head of the other guy. The one pulling the darts out was so wasted that he turned around and in a dazed whisper he said, "Ouch." The pain barely registered at all. He walked through the party with the dart stuck in his head.

When midnight came, all hell broke loose. About eight of us hit the street—four from our gang and four from the gang throwing the party. It was amazingly dark and still. The pent up tension was still there and it needed to come out. We had one purpose in mind—find something to destroy.

We walked a block or so and saw four college football player types leaving another party. Bingo. As they walked to their car, in a low and rough voice, Billy yelled, "What did you say?"

These guys didn't really say anything, but it was a good line to start something. They were much bigger, about five years older than we were, and they were also drunk. They weren't going to take any lip from a bunch of punks. One of them yelled back, "We didn't say anything." It was all we needed.

As we got closer, we were tensed and ready. The streetlights showed that three of them were white and one was black. We split up. Billy and another one of the guys moved in on the black guy. Billy got right in his face and started talking trash. This guy must have been six inches taller than Billy. I could tell this guy was intense, and I knew he was ready to explode. I stepped in between them and started negotiating. I was saying something about how we needed to chill out; we all had too much to drink. They weren't listening and instead both were staring a hole right through me. I could see the bloodshot whites of their eyes and felt their steaming breath as they were trying to hold back. Then it was too much—the thin line of peace was shattered. The pent up raw energy and fury was released in a full-on punch to my jaw. My teeth rattled, and my knees buckled, but I didn't fall. That was it. There was no turning back.

In an instant, Billy and another guy threw the black guy against a car, and I was pounding him in the head. I'd been here before, and instinct took over. I couldn't feel my jaw or anything except my fist hitting his head, over and over. I pummeled him until his lifeless body slid into the wet street. Knowing it wasn't over, I looked up to see fighting all around. Across the parking lot, one of the guys from the other gang had pulled out a knife. I ran over and said, "You don't need the knife. We're kicking their butts!"

He looked at me with cold, seething rage. His pupils were completely dilated and fixed as he said, "I want to kill a nigger."

I knew he had lost it and was not going to be stopped. I grabbed for the knife, and he stabbed me in the arm. He ran off into the night, and I stood there dazed.

The urgent screaming of the sirens broke the spell. Suddenly I was slammed back to reality. I felt the cold air, the exploding pain in my jaw and the open hole in my arm. We had crossed the line. The group disbanded and ran down the darkened streets as the sirens came closer. I didn't know what had happened to anyone except Buzz, who was black and blue running by my side. Were the others stabbed? Was anyone dead?

As we turned down a side street, I heard a cop pull up beside us. He hit his siren and flashed his lights. It stopped us dead in our tracks. My heart was pounding, my arm throbbed, and my mouth was lopsided and dry with fear. The cop rolled down his window wanting answers. "You boys know anything about the fight down the street?" he asked sharply.

This must have been our lucky night because it was Officer Jackson, a local cop we knew. We said we didn't know anything about a fight. We were just heading home from a New Year's Eve party. Jackson shined his flashlight on my arm and then back in my face. "How'd that happen?"

Looking down at my arm, he could clearly see blood seeping from the open wound. "We were coming from a party, and we crossed through some yards. I cut my arm on one of the fences we jumped," I said out of breath.

Jackson had been on the streets for years. He knew that I was lying; still, he let us go. We were so lucky. If he took us in, we would've been there a while with our previous records. When he left, we ran all the way to Buzz's mom's apartment where we crashed for the night. It was 1981—a new year. I wondered if I would spend time in jail because of that fight. Then I passed out cold.

Eventually, everyone in the gang was ordered to appear in court. This is where we heard the results of that night. When all was said and done, four people (me and three of the college guys) had been stabbed. The black guy was stabbed in the side multiple times. One of the stabbings was a quarter of an inch from his liver. He was lucky. A stab just a hair over or bit deeper would have killed him.

The guy with the knife was charged with attempted murder for stabbing the black guy. He was eventually convicted of a lesser charge but due to other crimes he ended up spending part of his life in prison.

South Side Scary

When the boys from the south side were together, it was a good bet that a fight would break out. Whether it was Mike beating a guy twice his size within an inch of his life with brass knuckles in a

White Castle parking lot, or Bobby who cracked a guy's scull with his cast in a fight. And then there was Billy, who didn't need any excuse. Once, we were high and we came across some guy doing his job, picking up trash in a movie theater parking lot. With no provocation, Billy just walked up and started punching the guy. We stopped Billy, but the damage was done. The guy was left lying in the parking lot buckled over in pain.

I always needed a reason to fight—like when someone messed with my family. Once, a so-called rival gang from the other side of town jumped my brother. He came to me and told me right after it happened. I immediately jumped in a car with some other guys and went on a hunt, but we didn't find him. Months later, we came across them in another car. In the middle of the road, we stopped and jumped out of our cars. Marty identified one of the four guys. Within seconds, my rage overwhelmed me and I continued to punch him on the hood of their car. Finally my brother and some of the others pulled me off of him. I didn't hear him at the time, but later I was told that he had been begging me to stop. I just blacked out with the rage.

> I would allow people to harass me, but I would not tolerate anyone causing my family pain.

I developed a bit of a reputation. Some high school kids came up to work and asked me to star in a short film they were doing for a school project. The film was about a loser who just didn't give a damn about life. It was loosely based on the Charlie Daniels song "Uneasy Rider" and probably was a lot like my life had become. They thought I fit the part well because I looked as wild as anyone could look. I think they wanted to get me on film before I self-destructed, and I was definitely on my way. They gave me a copy of the film when they were done. Like most other possessions in my past, it got lost.

There was a guy who lived in our neighborhood the kids called "Joe." He was a war veteran and a drug addict. The stories would start when we would see his daughter, who was only twelve years old, but very pretty and shy. They said this guy would get drunk and high on cocaine with his buddies. Then when the guys got good and buzzed, he would let them go into his daughter's room and have their way with her. There were also rumors of his arsenal of weapons. Everyone suspected him of several murders and wondered when he would lose it and kill again.

One day while we were hanging out, a car pulled up and the neighborhood kids let out a gasp. "It's him!" they whispered. He definitely looked like a Vietnam Vet—all decked out in his fatigues, unshaven face, and wild unwashed hair. He approached us with a blank stare on his face. He asked if we knew where he could score some drugs. Somehow he noticed me out of the corner of his eye and asked, "Who's this?"

"His name's Cooley," one of the kids said.

He walked up to me and without a word, he reached into his coat pocket and pulled out a 22-caliber pistol. "What do you think of my gun, Cooley?" he asked.

With a somewhat nervous response, I said, "That's a good-looking gun. Isn't it a Saturday Night Special?"

As soon as I said that, he pulled a .357 Magnum from inside his coat. In an instant, the steel barrel was against my head and he cocked the trigger. "What do you think of this one, Cooley?"

Smelling trouble, some of the kids ran off. I was sweating and panicked, but trying to remain calm. I was silent for a moment and could feel the cold steel push further against my temple. "That's a nice gun, too," I replied without any spit left in my mouth. He held the gun there for what seemed to be the longest twenty seconds of my life, not really knowing what to do. It's like he was battling with himself internally.

Finally, he pulled the gun away from my head and said, "You must really like guns. Come here, I want to show you something."

My knees were weak, my head ached from the strain, and my stomach was in knots. But just like that, I survived his gauntlet, and I became his good friend. We walked to his car and he opened his trunk. Sure enough, there was his arsenal of rifles and machine guns displayed before us. I wonder if the rumors about killing were true...

Chapter 6:

Busted Again, In More Ways Than One

Like some type of Jeckel and Hyde, whenever it was time for me to be at work I was there, giving a 100 percent to the job. I partied hard, but when it came time to work, I was there—body, mind, and spirit. I always worked hard and gave it my all. I should have spent more time at work.

Trying to just have one night doing what normal young boys and girls would do became way too complicated. There were a couple of girls that we met that were from the "right" side of the tracks, and we wanted to impress them. Acting like we had a car was a good start. After some begging, my sister's boyfriend gave in and let us borrow his car. The evening was great and just when I thought this could be the start of something good, everything changed in an instant. As we were driving home, we saw lights in the rearview mirror. We were being pulled over by the police. He pulled us over for not using a turn signal or something dangerous like that. I believe he would have let us off with a warning, but as he ran a background check, out came the guns, and more police. They surrounded the car; we were handcuffed and taken to jail. Eventually, we learned that my sister's boyfriend's wife had reported the car stolen because the boyfriend left her for my sister (confused yet?). It took some explaining, but eventually we got it sorted out. Needless to say, the girls from the right side of the tracks and their parents wanted nothing to do with us.

Snowed and Plowed

I'll never forget the night, it was just about 11:30 p.m., and I had just closed up the store. Buzz and three of his friends were waiting for me. I hopped in the car and discovered it was a party on wheels. They had five cases of beer (that's a case for each of us), and someone brought drugs. We spent the next three hours drinking, smoking dope, and dropping acid. This night, I dropped more acid than I ever had before. We drove all over St. Louis and drank every single beer—120 to be exact. We still wanted more.

We were higher than we had ever been and were driving like maniacs through the city when it began snowing. As a blanket of snow fell softly, we were tearing up the city with one purpose—alcohol. It was well after 3:00 a.m., and nothing was open. We ran out of places to find more beer, so there was only one thing for us to do, steal it! We stopped in the middle of the street in front of a neighborhood bar. All of us walked up and almost simultaneously we kicked the door. Since we were so loaded, all that happened was that we slid on the snow and landed flat on our backs.

Laughing, we got on our feet and charged the door only to bounce back—the locks and bars would not give. After several tries, we surrendered to the mighty door. We piled back into the car and drove off. We were just about ready to admit defeat when we passed by a grocery store and someone came up with a brilliant idea. (I use the word "brilliant" loosely.) We would use our car to get to the beer.

Behind the store, Buzz and two of the guys in the back seat stumbled out. It was snowing again and the whole car, including the windshield, was covered. We couldn't see a thing, but we could hear. We just sat there stoned out of our minds as the other guys took a tow chain out of the trunk and wrapped it first around the back bumper and then around the handles of the back doors of the grocery store. Buzz jumped in the back seat of the car and said, "Go!" The driver hit the gas, and the car took off. The chain locked straight and jerked at the back of the car; the tires spun in the snow. Buzz yelled again, "Go!" The driver hit the gas once more, but it had the same effect.

While everyone's attention was turned to the rear of the car, I glanced forward to see the white sheet of snow light up like Christmas. "Oh my God," I said. The others turned to the front to see the entire Second District Police Force surrounding the perimeter and closing down any chance of escape. Plus, we couldn't have got away anyway with that stupid chain hooked to the back of a store. This police department was known throughout the city as the toughest and most radical force in the city. Many citizens had died inexplicably, suffered greatly, or perished under this department's watch.

The sound of the sirens and then a bullhorn cut through the silent night. The voice at the end of the bullhorn ordered, "Get out of the car, and put your hands on top of the car." We quickly complied, and then in a strange move, they told us to get back in the car. I later realized they wanted to count how many people were in the vehicle.

As we waited, the snow had once again covered the windshield, and we couldn't see a thing. We could hear the cops yelling as they were chasing two of the guys that had been waiting by the door. I sat in silence. I was high and hallucinating when the door flung open and a hand reached in. The hand grabbed me by the hair and pulled me from the car. Without seeing the cop's face, I was turned back toward the car and he started hitting me in the head with his .357 magnum. I felt the back of my head start to crack open. He and other cops grabbed me and threw me to the trunk of the car. They forced my head down and put on handcuffs. The same cop started hitting me in the head again with his pistol. That small crack deepened into a valley in my skull; the blood was covering the trunk of the car. I couldn't take much more. I was getting ready to pass out when the cops grabbed me and lined me up with the others. One of the guys had managed to escape, and the cops were determined to find out who he was and where he was headed.

As I stood there dizzy and barely able to stand, about fifteen cops circled us. One of the cops spoke up and said, "Where's the other one?" No one replied, and then the cops started talking among themselves loud enough so we could hear. "Let's just kill all of them. I just don't feel like dealing with them. It would be easier to kill them and dump them somewhere." Of course, this was a scare tactic…or was it? We were so high and drunk we could barely stand or think.

The cop said, "Let's give them one more chance. Where's your friend?"

Being the bright guy I am, on the verge of collapse, I snapped, "We don't know!" Wrong answer. One of the cops stepped up and hit me in the back of the head with a slapjack. When this heavy steel ball wrapped in leather hit me, I fell to my knees. Instantly, I was jerked back up to my feet. We never told them who the fifth guy was, and they never found him. They also didn't kill us either. Eventually an ambulance showed up, and I was the only one who ended up taking a ride in it.

When I arrived at the hospital, I was taken in a back entrance and down to the basement. Lying on a stretcher, I was put in a line with other occupied stretchers waiting my turn. I was so out of it; I didn't know how long I would last. The acid had my heart beating like crazy, and I had lost a lot of blood. When I looked at the gurney next to me, realized that I could wait a little longer. He was a black guy with blood all over him. I later would find out from the doctor that he was stabbed to death in a fight.

Finally, I was rolled into a room. Very matter-of-factly, like I was a torn seam in a pair of pants, the doctor came and sewed my head up. Twenty stitches later, I was hauled off to jail.

When I arrived at the county jail, I went through an examination. I guess they were trying to make up for the one I didn't get at the hospital. I was strip-searched. It was a very complete process, and every orifice was checked. I was then fitted with the standard requisition orange jump suit prominently lettered with the name of this fine establishment: "City Jail."

My cellmate was a black guy who looked to be in his thirties. Feeling like it was a movie, and not real life, I opened with the common icebreaker in jail. "What you in for?" I asked him. He told me how he had been wrongfully accused of killing his wife and four-year-old daughter. He had been working on his rifle when it accidentally went off and shot his wife. The bullet then went through her and hit his daughter, killing them both. (I later read in the newspaper that this same guy was alleged to have brutally murdered his wife and daughter, shooting them both multiple times with a rifle. I'm glad I didn't know that at the time.)

After a sleepless night in the jail cell, I was ordered to appear in court. Handcuffed and shackled, I was shuffled into a courtroom with the other criminals as the judge heard our offenses. As I stood there in front of a courtroom, I realized that I must have been a horrible sight. I had not showered since the hospital, and I was dirty and smelly from the entire ordeal. My hair, which ran the full length of my back, was matted in dried blood. Part of the side of my head had been shaved for the stitches, which were clearly visible. There were about twenty jagged stitches poking out of my skull. Finally, my charges were read: second degree burglary and resisting arrest. Resisting arrest? I couldn't believe it! Without an opportunity to respond, I was led back to my jail cell.

Released and Repeating

Several days later, I was released on my own recognizance, and I was ordered to appear in court a few weeks later. The same night I got out of jail, I was partying like there was no tomorrow at a Ted Nugent concert.

When I showed up for court, I faced the cop who had beaten me senseless. I testified and told my story. His story for the stitches was that I had bumped my head crawling out from underneath a semi-truck where I had been hiding. To make it more believable, he should have at least said that the truck fell on my head. It didn't matter, I was a no one and I was found guilty. But again, since it was my first offense as an adult, I was given a year of probation.

> The beatings, stitches, jail time—nothing changed my life. I was continuing my same old ways with another typical evening of drinking, drugs, and hanging out.

About 2:00 a.m., the party started to wind down. Somehow, a few of us ended up cruising the deserted streets looking for trouble. We came across a typical neighborhood bar on the corner of one of the city's main streets. Mike and I jumped out of the car and ran up to the bar. Mike quickly used a crow bar to break the lock on the door and we were in.

Armed with our crow bar and heavy boots, we began a systematic process of breaking into cash registers and vending machines. As opposed to the guys I worked with on other burglaries, Mike was a professional—he did this for a living. We used our heavy coats as saddlebags and filled them with cash and change. Within minutes, we were done and were on our way out the door. Just as we stepped outside the door, we noticed a single car coming toward us on the main street.

Wouldn't you know, it was just our luck, a cop car making its rounds. As we froze, the cop spotted us and the chase was on. We ran around the back of a bar and into an alley; it was a dead end. We ran toward some stairs that headed up the back of the bar. As we reached the top of the stairs, the spotlights were already shining in our direction. We quickly shed our heavy coats. We fell to the deck at the top of the stairs and lay there quietly, hoping they would pass us. Again, no such luck as the light shined right on us, and the bullhorn announced that they knew we were up there and ordered us to come on down. We had no choice; we complied.

Another trip to the police station. This time, we met the owner of the bar. The man entered the police station and was understandably furious. Mike and I were handcuffed to the desk of the cops completing the reports. The owner of the bar came over and started yelling in our faces. I remained quiet and took my verbal lashing—I had had much experience with this treatment. The other Mike, not so much. He started cussing right back and then kicked the old guy jerking the officer's desk with him.

I was back in jail again, and this time it would cost me. I had used up my get out of jail free card and any luck I had during earlier escapades. My bond was set at $25,000. To get out, I had to come up with 10 percent; otherwise I would stay in jail until my court date. There wasn't a family member that could afford to help me. I would have to rely on my own savings to get me out. Working with my brother, he collected all my savings, my paycheck from work, and I still didn't have enough. Once again, God came through. Okay, maybe it was the IRS. My income tax check had just come. Marty was able to turn them all into just enough cash to bail me out.

And what did I do the day I was released? Went to a Rush concert. I thought I was invincible and continued to take risks with my life. I guess at that point, I didn't really care if I lived or I died. But one thing I knew for sure, just as certain as the day I stopped Peggy's abuse. I knew there was no way I was going back to jail.

All of us in the gang ended up in jail sooner or later. We were young and thought we were tough and invincible. I remember when the show *Scared Straight!* aired, and I happened to catch part of it. I wondered where they got those wimps! What a bunch of wusses! I'd like to see them try that with some real tough guys like me and the guys I hung out with. Yeah, we were real tough.

Chapter 7

...And People Died

Here is where it ends! There is that fork in the road. It is that last chance to change your course. I had plenty of signs to take a different road, but I didn't. Maybe things were so bad that I had a death wish. There is no way I should be here today to share this because I continued to ignore the signs. Someone greater than me must have had a different plan for me.

I don't know how we ended up meeting Tony, but boy, was he a piece of work. We ended up partying with him, and he told us that people called him "Disco." Tony was about twenty-two years old, six-foot-two, and 240 pounds. He had shoulder-length hair with a scraggily beard and mustache, a very unkempt-looking individual. He had a whole lot of energy and found some very mean ways to use it, which brings me to how he got the name Disco. Forget that his name just happened to be the same as the Saturday Night Fever star; Tony's nickname came from a more direct source.

Tony had just gotten out of the Army, where one of his accomplishments was a Golden Gloves Championship in boxing. His love for boxing was evident from the tattoo on his arm of a small boy in a boxing stance with big, oversized boxing gloves. The tattoo covered about three inches of the side of his bicep. One night, Tony was out celebrating his release from the Army at some discotheque. Tony and his friends had done a bunch of Valium and were drinking heavily. Eventually, Tony got out of control and he and his friends got into a fight with others at the discotheque. When the police arrived, Tony was out front fighting, apparently, taking out one person after another. When the cops came to try and break up the fight, Tony started swinging at the officers. He punched a female police officer in the face and knocked her out. Tony spent some time in jail for that move. From that day forward, those friends started calling him "Disco."

Disco used his size and intimidation to either be your friend or your enemy, and while it was dangerous to be his friend, you sure didn't want him as an enemy. Disco never seemed to have a job but could always come up with a little money. A lot of times I didn't know what he did, but I heard it wasn't legal. Sometimes I knew where his money came from—he bummed it from us.

Disco brought a whole new level of trouble to our gang. We could not go anywhere without running into an incident. His reputation grew quickly on the south side. And his bad boy image was just what Billy's sister, Patty, was looking for. They started dating shortly after he joined up with us. Of course Patty wasn't the only one he dated; he would cheat on her every time he got the chance.

Disco made a lot of enemies, and occasionally one of his enemies would have the guts to challenge him. One night one of the neighborhood tough guys, who was about the same size as Tony, ran into him at a gas station. He walked right up to Tony, talked some trash, and punched Disco right in the face. Tony barely moved and as he looked back at the guy he said, "You crazy S.O.B.," and hit the guy. This guy dropped like a sack of potatoes and lay there unconscious as Tony walked away.

Because of Tony's infidelity and his own insecurities, he was also very jealous of any guys that associated with Patty. One Saturday, all of us were at a carnival downtown. Tony and Patty got into an argument. The argument escalated to a point where Tony slapped Patty across the face right in front of everyone. Patty threw a beer bucket at Tony. It was at that point that Disco distanced himself from Patty.

Patty was hurt and humiliated. She was upset, and when I walked up to her and she flung her arms around me and cried on my shoulder. Suddenly, she pushed me back and whispered, "Here he comes." I turned just in time to meet his fist.

His punch landed dead in my face, and I fell to one knee. As I tried to shake off the blow, I looked up at and told him, "Tony, you're real tough, probably the baddest guy I have ever met. But one day, someone's going to come along that's going to be a little bit tougher and a little badder. Then you're going to see how it feels to hurt."

After I said my piece, he walked over to John, who had done nothing to deserve it and punched him in the face. Maybe Tony found out that John used to date Patty. Even though John and Patty dated years earlier, Tony just had to send a message.

After that, we parted ways. I would see Tony one other time, working at a gas station. He wanted to go out and party, but I declined. Eventually, what I said after our altercation years earlier turned out to be true—someone bigger and badder did come along. They found Tony on the side of a highway, and his face was unrecognizable. They knew it was him by his tattoo of the boy boxer. Tony had been shot in the face with a .357 magnum at point-blank range, execution style over a drug deal. Tony tried to rip off the wrong group of people.

During the investigation into the death of Tony, I ended up on the FBI's list to be interviewed. I decided it was a little too hot in town and hitchhiked my way back to Texas. They never found Tony's killers.

My teenage years were coming to an end. I'd spent the majority of that time hitchhiking back and forth between Texas towns and St. Louis. When I finally stayed in St. Louis, my mom was so out of control, I ended up being homeless much of the time. I decided I was on my own without a real family, so I started hanging with a gang. I perfected the art of partying—tried all kinds of drugs and hung out with really bad dudes. Since Mom couldn't deal with me, I went back to Texas and ultimately dropped out of school; I had a number of jobs during this time—a grocery store, mopping tar, moving stuff, washing dishes. The work was the most positive thing in my life so far. I worked hard and was rewarded with money, praise, and recognition. These good feelings of self-worth propelled me to do whatever job I had to the best of my ability. This was like a new drug for me—I was hooked. Despite all of the booze, drugs, family issues, I always made it to work. Maybe my old man's work ethic rubbed off on me after all.

Looking Back

I relive these times over and over in my head, and I still can't believe I lived through all these near-death experiences. Again and again, over and over, I repeated the bad choices that almost cost me my life. I was on the wrong path that was going to lead to my demise.

I was an awkward teenager feeling insecure trying to hide all my weakness through a hard exterior, alcohol, drugs, and violence. I needed something to believe in. I needed a purpose. I needed the right kind of mentor, and I am sure there were good mentors; I just chose to follow the bad mentors until it almost cost me everything.

If I had nine lives, I used the majority of them through these years, but I made it and it was for a reason. I just wouldn't know what that reason was until several years later.

SECTION 3:
YOUNG ADULT YEARS

Chapter 8:

Living Like A Rolling Stone

They say, "A rolling stone gathers no moss." In my late teen years and early adulthood, I rolled up and down the Texas to St. Louis corridor many times. I didn't stay in one place long enough to gather any moss or put down roots. It didn't seem like I'd ever settle in one place.

I can't count the number of times I hitchhiked back and forth from St. Louis to Texas. Most of the time, I was alone with my thoughts, my pain, and empty pockets. It was a tough way to travel, but I didn't have any alternatives. Many nights I stood in the pouring rain, in the red mud of Oklahoma. Or, I'd be waiting in the blazing heat or freezing cold for some kind soul to stop and pick me up. I usually didn't have any money, so I would survive by stealing food from stores or trying to bum money from those who'd pick me up. When the heat was too much, I'd borrow a hotel's swimming pool and jump in, clothes and all. This was a three-fer: I'd cool off, clean up a bit, and it was also how I would wash my clothes. When the nights got too long with no ride in sight, I'd lay my head to rest in the ditch beside the highway and sleep for a short time. Then I'd take my place on the highway's shoulder with my thumb out.

Life is a Highway

I met a lot of interesting people on my journeys and have many stories about those days. It's funny; most of the people that I met were just like me—searching for answers in bottles of booze or colored pills as they cruised the highway of life. It wasn't just young people either. Once I got picked up a couple of older mountain people in a souped up old Mustang. They were husband and wife and looked to be in their late forties. The guy had long gray hair with a long gray beard, and the woman had only a few teeth. They pulled out one of the biggest marijuana joints I had ever seen. I don't remember much of the trip after they dropped me off.

Another time, I was traveling with my friend, John. A clean-cut guy in his forties picked us up. He was driving a brand new Cadillac. Along the way, John and I were talking about the little sleep we had gotten and were wondering how we were going to stay awake. With that comment, the guy said he had something to take care of that and we pulled over at the next rest stop. We all got out and looked in his trunk. Before us was an entire pharmacy of drugs. He told us what each color was for and to take what we wanted. As we continued our trip, he told us he made his living as a drug dealer to truckers. He'd use his CB with code words to meet truckers at truck stops. There he'd sell them speed to keep going through the night. From the looks of his car and the way he dressed, business was very good.

Once on a trip to Texas when the rides got too far and in between, we'd had enough and went into a trailer park to look for a car to hot wire. This turned out to be unnecessary, because we found a Rivera with the keys in it. We took off, but we didn't get far because we ran out of gas and didn't have a dime to our names. We put the car in a ditch and started walking. It didn't take long before we were picked up buy a pair of dope smokers who had plenty to go around.

Another time I was picked up in Oklahoma City at about 3:00 a.m. by a guy about my age. He was just driving around the city late at night without much to do when he picked me up. He asked where I was heading, and I told him Texas. He said, "You know,

I'm not doing anything. I'll just give you a ride to wherever you're going in Texas."

We picked up some pot and speed and headed back to Gainesville. We were wired when we hit town, so my dad wouldn't let us stay there. With that, my new party chauffer drove us back to St. Louis. There I hooked up with my ol' girlfriend, Diane (will I ever learn?). She had a two-year-old child. We fired up on a bunch of speed, she dropped off her baby at her mom's, and the three of us were on our way to Florida to make our fortune. But first, our new friend had to pick up money, clothes and drugs from his mom's in OKC. When we got to his apartment, all hell broke loose. His mom had found his drugs, went berserk, and had the police waiting. Our recent dream was over. He was gone and Diane and I were stuck in the middle of OKC with no wheels. We stuck our thumb out and hitchhiked back to St. Louis.

Eventually, we made it back in one piece, she went back home to her mom, and I bounced around, staying with different friends and occasionally stayed with my mom. As you might have expected, eventually Diane and I went our separate ways

Putting Down Some Roots

Every time I'd get back to St. Louis, I would end up hanging out with the same old crowd. We would spend our time and what little money we had getting high and hanging out at parties. One summer day, we ended up at an apartment complex's pool party on the other side of the city. It was at this party that I met Linda in front of a keg of beer. I poured her a beer, and the rest is history. I ended up staying with Linda that night and for many nights to come. Linda had a job working for the state, so she worked during the day and we partied at night. She didn't have much money, but what she had we spent on alcohol and drugs.

I didn't have anywhere else to go, and she was doing everything that I asked. We were behind on our bills, so I told Linda to take out a loan for $500. Instead of paying bills, we spent it on our bad habits. We partied for three days straight and stopped when the money ran out. However, I did manage to find a job during one of those drunken binges.

I was bored, penniless, drinking, and walking the streets when I came across a couple of guys in back of an Italian restaurant smoking a joint. By looking at me when I walked up, they knew without a doubt that I wasn't the law or a narc. I was eighteen years old; I had straight, long hair nearly to my waist. I had an old pair of blue jeans on but no shirt or shoes. As I walked up with a beer in my hand, one of the guys asked if I wanted a hit. I didn't refuse, so I pulled up a piece of concrete and joined in. Eventually, these guys took a liking to me. A few hours later, they asked if I needed a job. "Sure—I can always use money." It was true, and I would do just about anything for it.

Cooking Up A New Career

Talanya's was an old Italian restaurant in the city that was trying to branch out to the suburbs. The place that I was going to work was its first attempt to franchise. The owner's name was Bud. He was a retired alarm manufacturer who took all of his retirement money and put it into this restaurant. He hoped to leave it one day to his son, Ed. Ed was a thirty-year-old spoiled kid whose mom and dad tried to build up the restaurant and then turn it over to him. Bud gave Ed a lot of control, including hiring responsibility. Ed was not ready for this, mostly because he was an alcoholic. Since the restaurant also served alcohol, this was not a good combination. Ed spent the day with a drink in his hand. He hired his wife, his friends, and recommendations of his pot-smoking friends. I was one of those "stellar" recommendations.

At first, Talanya's got some help from its established business in the city. They brought some of their people to help the place get off the ground. It was one of those people who showed me how to cook. The food was good, but it wasn't the only draw—partying and dealing drugs were always taking place during business hours.

It was unbelievable. Sometimes Bud would open up the bar, and we would drink his liquor until the sun rose. I believe Bud knew that in addition to drinking, we were doing cocaine, uppers, downers, and smoking plenty of marijuana, but he never addressed it. The sex was also ridiculous. Many of the people who worked there were married but were always sleeping with someone other than their spouse—this included Ed and Bud. It was hedonism at its highest degree, and because of this, the business was going down the toilet in a hurry.

I continued to live at Linda's apartment, so the partying was constant at home and at work. Linda's four-year-old daughter from a previous marriage, Jessica, also lived with us. We made a regular habit of dumping Jessica off with her grandparents, who were happy to take her. Linda truly loved her daughter, but the alcohol and drugs had a tight grip and had become of higher importance. Jessica and I began to develop a relationship during this time. Her father was not a part of her life then, and I guess she was looking for a father figure. I sure wasn't ready to be a father. Still, Linda, Jessica, and I formed a dysfunctional and misguided family unit. Because of this strange bond, everyone was pressuring us to get married and "settle down." My friends felt that it might make me more responsible and stop the downward spiral that my life had become with the booze and drugs. I had no intention of getting married, and there was nothing about my life that was ready for such a commitment, so Linda and I continued to live together.

Giving In

Just as I had done all of my life up to this point, I continued to battle between bad and good, right and wrong, being drunk or sober. There was one place where the battle did not take place—work. I worked hard at my job. I always took work seriously and put forth my best effort, regardless of the job. At Talanya's, I soon became the head cook. I was trying to reduce the partying and avoid trouble, but it's hard when everyone around you always wants to party. Eventually, I knew it wasn't going to work out between Linda and me. I started thinking about ending the relationship, but again, everyone was telling me that marriage was the key to staying out of trouble. After a while, I began to think that if Linda and I got married that she might settle down as well. So at eighteen, I proposed to Linda, five years my elder.

A few weeks before we got married, I moved in with a co-worker and friend, Stan, and his wife, for a bit. One day, as I walked up to Linda's apartment, I could see that my future wife was in the arms of another man. When I got to the window, the rage inside me reached a volcanic eruption when I noticed that the man was my best friend, Stan. I walked right up to and through the window. Glass exploded through the entire apartment. The broken shards of the window glass sliced into any skin not covered by clothing. My face and arms were covered in blood as a result of the broken glass. I just looked at the two of them as I was bleeding and dripping. Without a word, I turned around and walked back to Stan's apartment. As I entered the apartment bloodied, Stan's wife saw me and asked what was wrong. What happened? She continued to press, but I never told her what caused this situation. Eventually, the physical and emotional wounds healed. When they did, what did I do? I married Linda, and Stan was my best man. I guess I forgave, but I never forgot. After all, I hadn't been a perfect angel either during our courtship.

The wedding was held at a Baptist church, but the denomination was really irrelevant. We saw a church; we liked its steeple and got the preacher to do the service. Our immediate family and the wedding party attended the ceremony. The wedding itself was quick and pretty uneventful. It took about fifteen minutes. We were married; we paid the preacher his fee and never saw him again. This was not at all how I dreamed it would be when I got married. (You see ladies, even men dream of fairy tale weddings—we just won't admit it.)

The reception was held at the tavern where my mom worked as a waitress. (Working here allowed her a way to continue to drink and get paid for it.) The reception brought together all the people that were a part of making me who I was. My dad drove up from

Texas with my step-mom; my mother was there, my brother, my half-sister, old gang members, and people from Talayna's. There we all were, drinking, laughing, and having a good old time. Even during the fun of the reception, I heard those voices in my head telling me that this was a mistake because neither of us could change our ways. At eighteen, with the direction my life and Linda's drinking were taking us, this would be a colossal mistake. If only I had listened to those voices.

The next day, I ignored the warning voices and turned my attention to settling down and becoming a "family man." My new bride and I rented a house in a low-rent part of St. Louis. There, we made the attempt to start a life—Linda, Jessica, and me. The drinking and drugs continued. Linda never seemed to be happy unless she was doing one or the other. We were both working and continued to have money coming in, but we just couldn't get out of the financial hole we were digging for ourselves. The bills were piling up, right alongside the beer bottles and the drug paraphernalia.

A New Start

Not too much later, my dad called with a job possibility in the company he worked for in Gainesville. I got the job. I went to work as a machinist in a manufacturing plant. The plan was to stay with Dad and get some money saved, find a place, and then relocate my family to Texas. Everyone, including myself, felt a change in scenery might be just what we needed. A small town where we could get away from Linda's over-involved mother sounded promising. Jessica could go to school and be in smaller classes and most important, we could break away from the bad influences of the city and the people we associated with. Things seemed to be looking up. I now had a decent job with benefits, and I could really focus on building a family.

One afternoon, Peggy yelled that Linda's mom was on the phone for me. (Peggy had not changed a bit from her ugly ways, but I was no longer under her thumb. I was older, and she did not mess with me.) Linda's mom told me that Linda had been raped.

Horror ran through my body as she went on to explain that Linda was okay. I demanded to speak to her as the tears poured down my face. She told me that she went out for a drink, and some guys had followed her home and burst in the door and raped her for hours. I could not contain myself. I was screaming in pain at the thought of my helplessness to protect my family. Later, I learned the true details of the story. She had been blind drunk and the guys who kept buying her drinks were hitting on her. When she refused them, they followed her and didn't take "no" for an answer. She was raped but did not report it, because she felt everyone would think she had instigated the attack.

We packed up what little we had and moved to Gainesville. Maybe with time, we could put the nightmare behind us and start building a normal life. Linda and I moved into a small garage apartment and I went to work at Weber Aircraft on the second shift. Sometimes I would work overtime and have to work even later. Linda would stay home with Jessica during the day while I was at work. It didn't take long before Linda craved some activity. She tried to pass the time by walking down to my dad's house and drinking a beer or two with the family. As the days passed, one beer or two beers turned into a six-pack and then she would continue to drink by herself back at the apartment. By the time I got home, she was drunk and many times, an argument ensued.

The drinking got worse. Since we only had one car, she would drop me off at work and immediately go buy beer. One evening, she didn't show up to get me from work. I called several times and didn't get an answer. I was extremely worried and upset because I knew how drunk she would be. I managed to catch a ride with a guy leaving the plant. When I arrived home, the car was gone, but the front door was open. Inside I found a five-year-old Jessica asleep and Linda was nowhere in sight. The visual hit me—I was reliving the nightmare of my childhood but from a different perspective. When I left my mother and her alcoholic lifestyle, I had vowed never to be back in this situation, yet here I was.

As the sun started to rise, I heard the car pulling into our gravel drive. I went downstairs to find Linda sitting in the car completely drunk. I snapped and I grabbed her through the car window. "Where have you been?" I yelled. "Why didn't you pick me up? How could you leave your daughter?"

Linda could barely remember her name much less where she had been for the past several hours. I tried to get her help by signing her up for the local Alcoholics Anonymous meetings. Unfortunately, it wasn't long before she stopped going. I was out of ideas and felt there was nothing left for me to do. It was time for her to go back to St. Louis. A few days later, I sent Linda and Jessica back to live with her mother.

Our relationship didn't have a chance in hell, but I believed in the sanctity of marriage and was going to do everything I could to make it work—somehow. I was laid off from my job and was desperate, so I went to work for a company that manufactured fiberglass shower stalls. I worked the graveyard shift from 11:00 p.m. until 7:00 a.m. All night long, I would be sanding or drilling fiberglass shower stalls. At the end of my shift, I'd be exhausted. Before I could go to sleep, I had to wash the smell and the fiberglass from my body. As I ran the washcloth down my exhausted arms, the fiberglass needles penetrated my skin. I had to work hard to pick the fiberglass off me with fingers and knuckles that were bleeding from the sanding and the drilling. I'd have to endure this painful ritual every morning before I could go to sleep. Still every evening, I would be there on time and do the job the best I could and to give it my all. I was committed to saving some money and getting back on my feet.

Called Back

A month into the new fiberglass career, I received a call that would change the course of my life. My mom said she wasn't feeling well and needed to have a checkup and get some medicine to fix her. Less than a week later, my sister Donna called to say that Mom was diagnosed with liver cancer. The cancer was advanced, and she had less than six months to live. I packed my things and went back to St. Louis.

Linda and I got back together, and I moved back in with her. She was still living with her mother. I quickly got a job as a dishwasher at Denny's, once again trying to get some sort of life established. Even though I was quickly promoted to cook and then lead cook, there still wasn't enough money coming in. So when I got a call from Ed asking me if I would come back to work for him at Talayna's, I agreed but only on a part-time basis. I recognized that this was a toxic environment luring me back to the dark side. I needed the money but had to be very careful not to fall back into that same old trap.

Chapter 9:

In A Family Way

"In every conceivable manner, the family is link to our past, bridge to our future."
—*Alex Haley*

My mother's health was quickly deteriorating to the point of being bedridden. This once-proud woman was depending on others to change her bedpan. Someone had to be with her around the clock. She was blind and could barely hear our voices. Her body and mind were losing the will to live. Mom looked like a skeleton with thin yellow skin hanging loosely on her frame. The cancer had consumed her entire body. The only thing she could eat was popsicles. It's ironic how Mom had spent so much of her time over the years trying to lose weight while battling alcoholism. Now she was all bones and had gone longer than I had ever seen without a drink.

Jessica spent quite a bit of time by my mom's bedside. I remember watching Jessica as she would sit there just holding Mom's hand. One morning, not too long after we moved back, the three of us went to see Mom, but we were too late. She passed away in the night. My sister told me that the last word anyone would hear my mom say was "Jessica," as Mom was calling her to hold her hand during those final moments.

The funeral was the first time in about seven years I would see my half-brother, Ken. As a Baptist evangelist, he gave Mom's eulogy.

> I guess the gathering reminded him of how much he wanted to steer clear of our family and its mountains of problems and addictions. I can't say that I blame him; however, I couldn't escape this life. Now instead of dealing with two destructive families, I was part of a third messed-up family—my own.

When the funeral was over, Ken spent a few hours with us. I would not see him again for almost two decades.

Marty had been staying with my mom and after she died, he was evicted from her apartment. My life had been so full of challenges. I hadn't seen him much until Mom got sick. Fortunately, he had made some friends down the street and moved in with one of them.

Ready to Explode

As for me, I went back to north St. Louis and continued to work the two jobs and live with Linda and her mom, Jessica, and now, Linda's brother. Yes, all of us under one roof. It was always a powder keg with a short fuse just ready to explode.

After my mom passed away, more anger and pain was locked away inside, and I wasn't about to let it out. *As I had learned from previous and painful experiences in my life, it wasn't a good idea to let your pain and emotions show.* I was at a point that if I did let it all hang out, there was no telling what the effects would be. I didn't even shed a tear at my mom's funeral. This was something that Linda could not understand. One day, she lashed out at me for not crying at Mom's funeral. This was just one of many misunderstandings that Linda and I would have. She didn't understand me or what my life had been. She was focused on herself and drinking. It was apparent to us that our relationship was crumbling. While I dealt with the pain and troubles in my marriage by throwing myself into two jobs,

Linda was throwing herself into alcohol, drugs, and partying while her mom watched Jessica.

I was trying to do something, anything to get us out of Linda's mom's house. Again, I found myself in a situation similar to my childhood—not wanting to go home to suffer the verbal abuse and watch the non-stop drinking. Many of Linda's nights were spent drinking with her mom and discussing what a loser I was. When I got home after the restaurant closed, I'd have to endure the results of a night of "Mike bashing" from Linda while she was in a drunken stupor. Looking back, this must have been how my dad felt, first with my mom, then with Peggy. What an awful existence. I had never truly considered how bad his life was until I was living it. It sucked!

There wasn't much more I could take, and Linda knew that I was about to leave. Something stopped me. Linda was pregnant. This should have been the most fantastic news for a married couple, but for us, it was something that we were not prepared to handle. Neither of us individually or together was in a condition to raise a child. I knew this as the gospel truth down to the depths of my core. Raising a baby would be next to impossible for us. Still, when Linda delivered the news, I embraced it and tried to convince myself that this might bring Linda and me back together. I was determined to make this work.

Now, when I went into work, I worked even harder. I stayed later at both jobs, day and night. I was telling myself it was to get my family out of Linda's mom's house and start a new life, but in reality I was still running from the pain and drinking. Meanwhile, Linda continued to get more and more pregnant (like that is possible), and her emotional state became more and more insecure.

The insecurities and lonely nights became too much for her and she returned to her old ways. She had already been smoking while she was pregnant and behind the scenes she had started having a beer or two, then three, four, and more. Finally, the drugs went back into Linda and into our unborn baby. While I knew about her smoking and raised it constantly as an issue, I let it slide because I also smoked and didn't have room to talk. I even accepted the one or two beers, because it was so much better than before when she was always high or drunk. Unfortunately, it didn't stop at one or two beers, and it soon seemed that our baby was barely an afterthought. The more she drank, the more problems it caused between us. My God, I was living the hell of my mother's drinking all over again and wondering if our child would suffer the same kind of life that mine had been. The pressure, emotions, and drinking were more than I was able to bear many days. Still, I refused to quit. I had to make this work for the baby's sake. I gave it my all.

A Final Straw

As things were going from bad to worse, one of my jobs was also coming to an end. Bud had had enough and was closing the doors. His dream of having his own business and passing it on to his son would not come to pass. Bud was broke, and Ed was drinking more than ever. Bud's wife was ready to leave both of them. Since he didn't want that, he conceded that he had made a mistake, closed the restaurant, and went back to work. Bud would try to build his life back at the age of sixty-five. Talk about a kick in the gut.

Just an hour from closing on the last night at the restaurant, Linda called. She was drunk and about six months pregnant. She started yelling and ordered me to come home right then! (I knew her mother was a party to her drinking that night and the recurring discussion about what a loser I was. Most likely, she planted this ultimatum in Linda's head.) My explanation about having one hour before I would be home fell on incoherent ears. She exploded. "You come home right now or don't bother coming home, ever!"

I took her words to heart. I never went home. I had had enough, and I knew that it was over. I just couldn't take it anymore. I was tired of the drinking, the drugs, the fighting, and Linda's mother. Eventually, I went back to pack some clothes. *As I drove away there was one little thing I forgot—I had no place to go and no money. My living hell just went from bad to worse.*

I began to live out of my car and slept at a rest stop between North St. Louis and Illinois. I would wake up in the morning and use the rest stop restroom to take a sponge bath and get ready to go to work at Denny's. It was tough making it to work every day, but that job was the only point of my existence. I still kept in touch with Linda and wanted to be there for her through her pregnancy. It seemed like I was blacklisted, and no one wanted anything to do with me.

Several weeks had passed, and I was still at the rest stop. I did manage to find a place to take a shower and wash my clothes a few times. My buddy Kurtis's parents were out of town for a couple of weeks, so he would let me come by and use his home to get ready for work. One day, Kurtis' parents came home early from vacation. His dad, who was a big man with a big attitude, came through the front door and literally threw me out, cursing me all the way. Kurtis would later tell me that his dad didn't like me because I left my pregnant wife. I guess the one-sided story of my abandonment traveled to a multitude of people.

Not making much more than minimum wage, my paycheck wasn't enough to get a place, but it did allow me to stay in a hotel room for a night or two. The hotel was just a block from skid row, so it wasn't exactly the Taj Mahal. Occasionally, friends would let me stay with them for a night, but they were now fed up with me too, and stopped answering the door. I was starting to believe what everyone had been saying about me: I was a loser.

Down On My Luck

At some point, my sister took pity on me and agreed to let me stay with her for a while. Luck was still not on my side. One evening after work in the middle of a heavily traveled road, my car just stopped moving. It was obvious that the transmission had gone completely out. There in a very questionable part of town, I left my car and walked to Donna's place. Fortunately, I had moved what little belongings I had to the apartment, because it was the last time I would see my Cutlass.

I ended up buying a beat-up, powder blue, 1973 Hornet that cost me a grand total of $200. People dubbed my new transportation the "Smurf Mobile." I had to finance it because I didn't even have that much money.

Donna was just as broke as I was. She was living with a big black guy named Terry. They made their way by hustling the streets of St. Louis and running a small prostitution ring out of their apartment. Their place was in a prime location for such a business. The girls would just come by with their "Johns" and give Donna and Terry money or drugs to use their place for about an hour. Donna would make me hit the streets until it was time to come back. As I left, I'd see the prostitutes waiting for the coast to be clear so they could do their business.

Donna and Terry also had their own drug-dealing racket. They would sell any kind of upper or downer they could get their hands on. Still, they never had any money and could barely make rent each month. Very seldom was there food in the apartment. The only thing that I could remember eating for a month was bologna. My skills in the restaurant industry helped me be creative. I had bologna every way you can imagine, fried, rolled, cold, and if we were really lucky, I sometimes had bologna with bread. I was really the only one worried about eating. Donna and Terry didn't seem to eat very much, and it was obvious why. They were addicts to the drugs they sold. They were only concerned about making enough money to support their habit.

I was twenty-one years old and right in the middle of it all—drugs, sex, prostitution, shootings, and murder. I was at great risk of becoming a product of my environment.

This was also where I was when my daughter was born.

On March 5, 1983, Linda had Amber. I was only a block away, but as fate would have it, it could have been the other side of the ocean. The day before Amber was born, I came down with the chicken pox. On her birthday, I had a fever of 103 degrees. I called the hospital and asked if I could come and see her; their reply was for me to stay as far away as I could. Not only was I dangerously sick, I was emotionally devastated at this latest blow.

After Amber was born, I stayed close for another year, but Linda and I were really having a difficult time with our relationship. We could not even be civil to each other. I'd receive calls at all hours of the night when she had been drinking. When it should have been a joy for me to go see my daughter, I would dread it because I would have to deal with Linda and her mother. I never could really bond with Amber, but I at least knew that Amber had a family—the one thing I could not provide. In addition to Linda and her family, down the street was Linda's other brother and his family and an aunt and uncle. I felt some sense of comfort knowing that Amber would be near relatives. I never really had a family or relatives, but I knew how important it is. These were the reasons I let go. I knew the type of life I was destined to live, and I would never be able give Amber any family to grow up with.

Staying at Donna's was getting to be a little too much for both of us. She didn't feel comfortable as she continued trying to hide what she was doing, and it was getting difficult for me to continue to act like I didn't know what was going on. My brother was also having some struggles of his own with his roommate, so he decided to get his own place. Eventually, I moved in with him to help share the cost of rent. I was still working at Denny's on the far north side of the city.

Partying With Marty

Even though Marty and I hadn't lived together since we were kids, our lives seemed to take parallel paths. We were both still partying as hard as ever. As the partying became more intense, so did the risks associated with this lifestyle.

After being completely smashed during a concert that ended after midnight, we went to my car, an old black '64 Impala (the Smurf mobile was no more). I was the designated driver (scary is an understatement). We decided we needed more alcohol. The only place we could afford to get any liquor at that time of night was East St. Louis. By many accounts, East St. Louis is considered one of the most dangerous places in the country, let alone the city or state. And it was even more dangerous to a group of white kids coming to buy alcohol on the "black side of town."

As we were driving, our attention was drawn to some female hitchhikers on the side of the road. I slammed on the brakes but since my motor skills were impaired, we had actually gone way past them before the car stopped. From the back window of my car, we watched them run toward us as our fantasies ran wild of what they might look like. As we waited, we noticed a car coming down the four-lane freeway. Its headlights were getting bigger as it approached. Buzz said, "I don't think this car is going to get over."

"Of course he is. The guy's got four lanes." Famous last words.

Suddenly the headlights were right on us, and I hit the accelerator. Too late. We felt the impact of the car hitting us and catapulting us over the curb and into the grass. The back window shattered with the impact. The steel trunk of the car was smashed all the way to the backseat, and two guys in the back came crashing into the back of the front seat. We had just been rear-ended by a car doing sixty miles an hour while we were at a dead stop.

We thought the driver was hurt because he stepped out of his car, fell, and rolled over right in the middle of the highway. When we went to check on him, we discovered he was "falling-down" drunk. When all was said and done, we lost the girls, I totaled my car, and we all got banged up, but no one died. This must have been what, my sixth car? One stolen, one left at the drive-in, one abandoned on the highway with the transmission falling out, three totaled due to drugs and alcohol.

> You would think that I would have read that big, bold danger sign and done something about it. I was back to my old ways and barely noticed.

The only thing that kept Marty and me from getting into more trouble was that we worked different shifts, so we couldn't be around each other all the time. Still, the partying intensified. We lived in a four-apartment flat, and everyone in the place partied. From the girl upstairs to our gay neighbor, there was a party every night. It would not be uncommon for one of us to be asleep and the other one would come home at 5 a.m. with a group of people, and a party would break out. While the drugs were not as hard they had been, there was still plenty of dope around. Once we had an entire duffel bag stuffed with marijuana. We sold some of it but smoked the rest. We were small-time drug dealers—the real drug dealer was our neighbor upstairs, Stephanie.

Stephanie told us about this huge dope deal she had in the works. She was negotiating a deal that would be worth a few thousand bucks. A few nights later, the deal was to occur, but something went terribly wrong and the people she was dealing with ripped her off. The next thing I know, six of us were on our way to the other side of town to take back what we believed was ours. We were packing guns and knives. On the way, we got braver and braver. Our adrenaline was at its peak when we pulled down the street from the house. We jumped out of the car and headed up to the house with our weapons drawn. Stephanie was the driver for what we believed would be a quick getaway.

We circled the broken-down shack, and one of the guys jumped up into a tree to see how many were inside. To our surprise, there was no one in the place. So we immediately kicked the door in. I went back to tell Stephanie we were in and taking everything we could get our hands on. Suddenly, we noticed the headlights of a truck pulling up in behind the house. Our guys would have never seen this truckload of guys pull up, if it wasn't for Stephanie sounding her horn. That move attracted the truck's attention to our vehicle and the shooting started. Stephanie stepped on the gas. We ducked as they shot at our car and we sped off. As we circled the block, we were panicked. There was no way I could leave without my little brother. I was frantic, not knowing if he had been shot or if they got him and were torturing him.

We were about to circle back when those familiar lights and sirens appeared behind us. The police pulled us over. Our hearts were racing. We watched as the officers slowly walked up on each side of our car. The officer leaned over on the driver's side and asked, "How are you doing this evening? I need to see some ID."

Seemingly satisfied with our proof of existence, he asked if we knew anything about the shooting that occurred around the corner. Our reply was consistent. "Shooting? What shooting?"

With a slight glare, he asked us to step out of the car. He then asked us to step to the rear of the car and asked, "Then how did this get here?" The trunk of the car had fresh bullet holes from a 30/30 rifle. We were caught dead to rights, but neither of us caved. We acted as if we didn't know how it got there. The officer asked us to open the trunk, so Stephanie did. As they traced the bullet's path, they found that it exploded a case of oil in the trunk, and then went through the back seat of the car, and the bullet finally came to rest in the back of the front seat.

> If the bullet had traveled a few more inches it would have struck me in my lower back. The officers told me how lucky I was. At that moment, wondering about Marty, I didn't feel so lucky.

The officers finally let us go with one requirement, if they saw us back in the neighborhood where the shooting occurred, they would assume we knew more than we did and arrest us. As the police followed us, we cooperated and went back to our part of town. Waiting to hear some word on my brother made for one of the longest nights. Later that morning, we heard from Marty and everyone had made it away safely.

My life had been out of control for years now, and it didn't seem like anything was going to bring me back. We were always into one trouble or another—drinking, driving, drugs, fights, robberies. It was not uncommon for the police to show up at our door, looking for one of us and if it wasn't for something we had done, it was for suspicion. They knew our number well. Out of the blue, I received a call from my dad in Gainesville. He told me that I had been called back to work by Weber. I almost dreaded the thought of going back to Gainesville, but something told me that I would not be long for this world if I remained in St. Louis. So I packed up, told my daughter good-bye, and headed south. Out of left field, I asked Kurtis if he wanted to come with and he said, "Sure." So we hit the road to Texas.

Chapter 10:

Perpetual Party Time

They say everything's bigger in Texas. The parties in Gainesville were a lot different from those in St. Louis—normally they were bigger and involved more booze. The really big parties were usually on somebody's farm way out in the country. One night, we ended up at such a party. We joined in on some of the heaviest drinking I have ever done in my life. People were drinking straight from a keg of beer, challenging each other to see who could drink the most. Others were passing around bottles of Tequila to see who could get to the worm the fastest. The aroma of marijuana filled the air. What a place to be.

The party attracted people from all over. Finally, when we were about as drunk as we could be, Kurtis and I decided to head back to town, smart huh? We eventually made it and headed for a spin down the drag. There is a point in the road where all cars follow a roundabout to go in the other direction. That's where we ran head on into another car. Kurtis was convinced he had the right of way, so he didn't even slow down, which the turning car expected us to do. Again, we were banged up but alive. Before I knew what was happening, Kurtis was out of the car and in the face of the other driver. The guy admitted fault and the world was right with Kurtis—at least for the moment. He was devastated when he finally saw the condition of his tricked-out Dodge. He spent the next few weeks finding the parts to rebuild his car. Eventually he got it back in one piece.

Candyland

A few days later, we heard from a couple of ladies we'd met at the party. It wouldn't take long before we would find out some interesting facts about them. The one Kurtis was seeing was married and much older than he was. But Candy, the one I was with, turned out to be eleven years my senior. Despite the age difference, a relationship had begun. It didn't take long for the lady that Kurtis was seeing to call it quits, because she felt guilty having a husband and a child. Candy and I became an item. Like all the others, she was a partier, and we spent a lot of time drinking and doing drugs. I wasn't looking for anything serious. In fact, after the disappointment of my failed marriage, I didn't think I would ever have a serious relationship again.

I was back to work at Weber as a drill press machinist. That means for eight to ten hours a day, I drilled holes. It was terribly boring, but it was an income. I often came to work high, which was a problem from a safety standpoint. But I was a dependable employee who always arrived on time and worked whatever overtime they needed.

About a year in to the position, an opportunity presented itself. The company started a group with the mission to work on ways to improve quality throughout the product lines. I was invited to join and I thought, *What the heck, anything that gets me off this assembly line for a while.* To do this, we met once a week for about an hour and half and brainstormed ideas on ways to improve quality. From the ideas came change and from the changes came positive improvements throughout the plant.

Surprisingly enough, I was quickly involved and excited about what we were doing. One of the things I particularly enjoyed was taking field trips to see how other companies were improving the quality of their products. One place we visited was French's (the mustard maker) in Sherman, Texas. This company was years ahead of Weber in processes, and we got some good ideas from that trip. I continued to get more involved in the Quality Circle Group and was afforded more time away from the line. It wasn't long before the group elected me to replace the Quality Circle Group Leader. I was a leader and having a good time at work. How'd that happen?

Trying to Get Ahead

This small success got me inspired to do things to better myself. Whenever Weber would offer any kind of additional training, I would jump at the opportunity. I took advantage of a blueprint reading course they offered and became certified in blueprint reading. I also wanted to take a GED test. Before I took the test, I had to do a few weeks of studying, since it had been so long since I had been out of school. And even when I was in school, I wasn't there mentally.

Only two people in my entire family ever earned a high school degree—my two stepbrothers. I studied as hard as I could and confronted my biggest fear in school—math. After a few weeks, I didn't feel my brain would absorb any more so it was now or never—I was going to pass or fail. The fear of failure was a prospect that I was unwilling to accept. I *had* to pass. When I finished the test, I waited impatiently for the teacher to finish grading. He told me I had passed and went on to say that my test scores in math were some of the highest he had seen in some time. *Well imagine that,* I thought to myself.

As I got more involved with the company, I made new friends. One of those new friends was a black guy named Ronnie. He was a partier, so away from work we did what we did best. In the early '80s, Gainesville was a small Texas town with deep racial segregation. So a white guy hanging out with a black guy always made people a little tense. To Ronnie, it just wasn't a big deal, and for me, blacks were as much a part of my life as whites. I was basically colorblind until I saw how others reacted when we were together. Ronnie and I just didn't care, and it made for interesting weekends.

It wasn't unusual to see Ronnie and me in an all-white cowboy bar. To make things even more interesting, Ronnie and I would go from pool table to pool table, taking all their money by beating them at pool. When these bars would shut down for the night (about 2:00 a.m.), we'd be headed over to the dark part of town. We'd go to a neighborhood lined with broken-down shacks. Inside, the only light came from one forty-watt light bulb hanging in the center of the bar over the pool table. You could make out the shapes of people but in that light, you couldn't tell who anyone was until you were up close. Whenever someone came near me, they recognized I was a white boy. I guess they thought I was out of my mind to be in the place. Little did they know how close to the truth they were.

I made a few friends in that neighborhood. I was often the only white guy playing a game of bad basketball in a dirt lot with a rusty hoop hanging from a tree branch. I never had a problem there because our respect was mutual.

Yes, I had all kinds of friends; I didn't have a problem with color. I would hang out with pretty much anyone. I felt that with all my own problems it wasn't my place to judge others. I was just happy to say I had friends, fair weather or otherwise.

In my personal life, I was getting more serious with Candy. It didn't take long before I was sleeping over and eventually living under the same roof with her, and oh yeah, her thirteen-year-old daughter. Candy also had two brothers and a mother—none of them were married. To say Candy's family was a little bit country would be a gross understatement. They were nothing but backwoods, and it took all of us some time to adjust. Eventually, we warmed up to each other, and we grew into one big dysfunctional family. Candy and her whole family were drinkers, and one of her brothers was a real dope smoker. This brother was also a real moocher and was always getting cash, dope, and beer from Candy. Once again, I was in an addictive relationship that was leading toward disastrous results.

Cranked Up

Once again, the drugs we did continued to intensify. Candy and I were hanging out with people who were selling just enough to support their habit. One weekend, a bunch of us from Gainesville went to a birthday party in Dallas for a guy I'd gone to school with. He was turning twenty-five years old, had been married for a couple of years, and had two kids. Our "pre-party" started in Gainesville with drinking and some acid. We then took the trip to Dallas in both our heads and in two cars. We finally found Ricky's apartment. The party moved to the next level as the alcohol and drugs got heavier. Needles made their appearance, and everyone was high out of their minds. My old buddy Larry was in the sauna having sex with his new wife as passersby looked in, but no one really cared—we were too busy dealing with our own trips. Candy and I ended up bonding with Ricky and his wife and would hang out with them again. Whenever we did, the needles came out again and we were into a new drug called "crank."

My brother had moved back to Gainesville, and he knew the term "crank" too well, as he was one of the leading dealers in town. Crank had become more than something to do for Marty—he was hooked. He sold as much as he injected. Both my brother and I were using way too much and were quickly approaching the end of the road, but we just kept pushing the pedal to the metal. We weren't dead yet but at the pace we were going, it wouldn't be long.

Candy and I were arguing more than ever. We had been together going on two years, and I think we were both getting bored. At almost thirty-four, she wanted to party more; I was pushing twenty-three and was getting tired of the partying again. I tried to focus on my job. Candy's boredom with me reached a point where she just wouldn't be home when I'd get off work. One night when she wasn't there I went to look for her. I went to her friend Pam's nice little suburban home and knocked on the door. Pam didn't know where Candy was. When I continued to ask a few more questions, I heard her husband yelling to close the door in my face, or he was going to come and kick my butt. I yelled back. I was already upset and didn't need his attitude. I saw him coming down the darkened hall toward the front door. He was a little bigger than me, and I could see he was carrying a large belt with a license plate-sized buckle. He swung the buckle my way. I met his arm and spun him to the ground. In my fury, I had snapped again. From there, I punched him repeatedly in the face until he begged me to stop. I came to, got into my car, and left.

I headed back to the house. On the way, I saw Candy's car drive by. I did a 180 and chased after her. I cut through some parking lots at high speed in my attempt to cut her off. She never saw me until I finally caught up to her in the driveway of her house. I came flying into her front yard and without even knowing it, I had brought some company. Two Gainesville police cars were right behind me. I jumped off my cycle and met Candy before she could get to the house. I demanded to know where she had been. She'd been with Dan (her ex-boyfriend). She then told me that he was passed out on the couch in the house. It was obvious from looking at Candy that they had taken a large dose of Valium. Once again, I lost it and walked up to the door and tried to kick it in. It was about that time the cops yelled, "Hey, you can't do that!" So, I walked out into the yard, and we had a discussion about the incident. I calmed down, and they let me go.

That would be the last time Candy and I would be an item. I knew it was another mistake, and the only way to break out of the relationship was for me to walk away from it. She continued to try to get back with me, but it wasn't going to happen. My heart was hardened by this point by all of the women in my sordid life. A hard, black, empty pit replaced what once had been open to love.

Living to Party

My life was totaled. I had no one of significance in my life, and I was living in an efficiency apartment just barely making ends meet. *I had lost my drive to do anything.* Partying had become a necessity instead of something to do. I needed it. The only "friends" I had partied, so I was getting drunker and higher than ever. I would be the first one at the party and the last one to leave. I became a joke. For my brother's birthday party, I came over at four to help him set up kegs of beer, bottles of whiskey, and the drugs. By the time the party started at 10:00 p.m., I was wasted and useless. One of the guys that showed up was Daryl. He knew I was sleeping with his ex-girlfriend, and he wanted her back. He just sat back and watched me get blasted out of my mind, and when the timing was right, he made his move.

Somehow he got me from the party to the side of the house in the dark where no one could see. We started having a discussion about his ex-girlfriend. I said my piece and turned to walk away when he hit me in the temple and I dropped. For a moment, I was out. When I came to, I felt Darryl and his friend kicking me in the face, ribs, and everywhere else they could. I couldn't fight or stand because I was too out of it. Out of nowhere came Marty, who pushed the other guy to the side and leaped on Daryl's back. He and Marty traded blows for a bit, and then Daryl ran off. It was just like the incident much earlier when David had me at a disadvantage and Marty came to my rescue. Since then, I had looked after Marty. Things had changed so much since then. *My life had reached a new low when my younger brother, the crank addict, had to look after me.*

That was the first time I ever remember losing a fight. Under the pretense of chasing after Daryl, I left the party. I knew I was barely alive. At my apartment, I was in the bathroom convulsing with dry heaves while my head spun so much that I couldn't see.

The next morning I woke up on the bathroom floor lying in a pool of my own vomit and blood. Another new low.

Chapter 11:

Looking For A New Beginning

I've heard the saying, "When one door closes, another opens." At this point in my life, I was looking for a way out of my current lifestyle. I'd take a door, a window, a crack in the wall—anything. These were desperate and lonely times. I was ready to give up.

After the incident with Daryl and the breakup with Candy, my so-called friends started to disappear. Both Daryl and Candy had lived around Gainesville for a long time and had a big influence on others.

One weekend, Butch, a buddy of mine that I worked with at Weber, and his wife, Lana, invited me to go out to Lake Murray, Oklahoma, for the day. Of course I had nothing better to do, so I made the trip. And I'm glad I did, because I finally met someone who meant something. I remember I saw her floating on a raft out in the water. I had been drinking and was feeling bold, so I swam out to her raft; as I got closer, the more beautiful she looked. She had the longest blonde hair I had ever seen and when I got close enough, she also had the most beautiful blue eyes I had ever seen.

I floated up and I said, "You're not from Oklahoma, are you?"
And she said no.
I said, "You're from Dallas, aren't you?"
She said, "How did you know?"

I said, "Because that's the only place they can make girls that look as good as you." Okay, so it's a pretty bad pick up line, but she laughed. I introduced myself, and she told me her name was Julie. We talked for a few minutes, and the next thing I knew, we were going out on a date the following weekend.

So Great

So the following weekend came, and I was really excited about this date. So excited was I that I borrowed a friend of mine's custom van. I wanted to impress Julie, and what I was driving wasn't going to impress anyone. I thought that a nice vehicle and a sharp dressed man (yes, I even put on a tie) would surely impress her. I was on my way to Dallas. After getting some less-than-correct directions that led me two hours out of the way, I finally reached Julie's parents' house about 11:00 p.m. As I suspected, her parents were conservative looking living in a conservative looking house. Her dad was an engineer for Rockwell, and her mom was a nurse. I thought to myself that this is a good girl, and I had better watch my P's and Q's.

It was midnight before we finally left to go out, and we went to one of the few restaurants that was open at that hour. We ate and got to know each other a little better. After we finished eating, we went to a club that was close by. That's where she told me that when she met me she thought I was Hispanic. I was so "loaded" when we met, and when I drink, my lisp is really prevalent, she thought I had said my name was Miguel Julio. My dark complexion made me look Hispanic. She was a little nervous about how her parents would react to their little white-bred girl dating a "Mexican." If they would have only known my past, they might have wished I was a "Mexican." All things considered, the night was a tremendous success. Julie and I hit it off instantly; in fact, we hit it off so well it was scary to me.

The following weekend, we were to see each other again, and I couldn't wait. My dad was going to take me to Dallas to look for a new car. My goal was to pick up the car and then go see Julie. We talked to each other several times during that week, and the anticipation of being together increased. That weekend, I purchased a 1982 Chevrolet Camaro. This was the newest car I would own, being only three years old. Now, I could feel proud to show up at Julie's house in my own vehicle instead of borrowing someone else's vehicle.

When it came time for me to go see Julie, I started questioning myself. *What are you doing? You don't deserve her. You're going to ruin a perfectly good girl's future. You are just not meant to be with someone like that.*

My low self-esteem convinced me to turn my car around and head back home without even calling about the change in plans. When I got home, Julie called again and again. I sat in my small apartment, listening to every message she left on the answering machine. Even though it was tearing me apart inside, I refused to pick up the phone. Days went by, and she continued to call and leave messages and then I thought she was done calling so I made the mistake of picking up the phone, and she was on the other end.

After she let me have it for a good fifteen minutes, I tried to explain what was going on in my head. And then something happened that I never expected, she understood. She was just about ready to say good-bye, and I was sure it would be the last time I heard from her and then I did a 180. I didn't want to lose her, even if it was wrong. I had never felt what I was feeling and didn't want it to stop. Not even realizing it, a single word flew from my lips, "Wait!" This was the one word that would begin a relationship and change my life forever.

Julie and I began our long-distance relationship. We'd drive back and forth to see each other as much as we could. I started to meet her friends, and we would go out on the weekends. Eventually her friends, who had their own places, would let me stay with them on the weekends. Then bright and early Monday morning, I would drive some seventy miles to be at work by 7:00 a.m. The desire to see each other more than just the weekend continued to grow to the point that I would drive up during the week. I would get off work at 3:30 p.m., and drive for an hour and half, stay with Julie and get up at 5:00 a.m. and drive back to Gainesville and be at work by 7:00 a.m. Finally, I was dating someone who was not related to my past, and she didn't even know about it. I could be the person I thought I was and not what the environment around me had chosen me to be.

Working with a Purpose

I was doing my best to get ahead in my job, so I could make enough money to spend more time with Julie. I was trying to move to the next level on my job. To do so, I had to take a test. I studied all I could about being the best press operator ever, and when the day came to take the test, I was comfortably positive that I could pass it. I walked into a room with four managers in white shirts and ties. As I sat in a chair, they began to ask questions. Even though I was nervous and wasn't feeling comfortable, I was doing okay answering the questions. Then, the bottom fell out when they started asking me questions that weren't even related to my job, department, or to my end of the plant. Weber employed up to a thousand people in many different departments, and there was no way I could know everything about every department. When they were done, I was a beaten man. I knew I didn't pass the test, and I didn't.

Later I spoke with a supervisor who told me that he knew I wouldn't pass the test either. It had nothing to do with my abilities or me. Clifford told me that they had already reached their quota for promotions in the department and while they can't keep people from applying for promotions, they can make the test to difficult for anyone to pass. This made me angry, and I knew it was just a matter of time before I was gone. Suddenly, Dallas seemed closer than it ever had before.

One morning after spending the night at Butch and Lana's apartment, they sat down with me and asked if I wanted to move in with them and take their spare bedroom. They said they knew I wouldn't have a job right away, so I could pay them when I had some money coming in. I jumped on the offer and packed up again what little belongings I had and moved to Lewisville, just north of Dallas.

I can still remember how excited and scared I was at the same time. I was going to move to the big city, to a city that was even bigger than St. Louis. I was going to be closer to Julie. I had no job, no money and no plan for how I would survive but I had been in this place before and I was determined to make this happen. But as with almost everything in my life, it would not be easy. This new mountain I was about to climb would be high and rocky and many times, I would want to just stop climbing and let go for a free fall.

My first so-called "job" in Dallas was a test to see if I was willing to pay my dues. I remember I fell victim to a hustle that many others had succumbed to, but it only took me a few weeks to figure it out. The job was advertised as a way to make big money and sold to people as a Smith & Barney Company. I really liked the company's tagline; I felt it was me, and I'm sure it hooked a lot of others in because by using the Smith & Barney name, people trusted them. And the tagline that inspired me, maybe you recall it: "We make money the old-fashioned way. We earn it."

After days of sales coaching, videos, and whiteboards, graphs, and charts, I finally found out they wanted me to sell vacuum cleaners! I am sure that many have built a good living from selling vacuum cleaners, but it wasn't for me. It wasn't that I didn't think I could sell; in fact, I had always believed that I could sell anything with only one prerequisite—I had to believe and trust in the product and the company I was selling for. The day I found out what we were selling, I left the office never to return.

I didn't get paid during this time, and it was another real setback. I was frustrated. I had been at Butch and Lana's for a couple of months, and it didn't seem I would be leaving anytime soon. Also, I still had no income to pay them. They never complained, but I know they had to be getting frustrated too. For me, it was back to the drawing board, and I hit the pavement again, looking for any job I could find. I was getting a little desperate because not only was I unable to pay Butch and Lana, but my new car payment was due again and I was running out of money. Just when I was about to throw my hands up, I walked into a lumberyard and got an opportunity at the ground floor level. That was all I needed—a chance.

> I was going to take full advantage of this opportunity because I was hungry. I was going to prove myself in this job at every level. I would not fail—I couldn't. I knew that too much of my future was riding on this.

The Hole

I recall one temporary assignment I had years earlier. I was there bright and early, not knowing what exactly I would be doing. I showed up in my cleanest, newest clothes, thinking maybe if they saw how professional I looked, they would have me do something in the front office. I quickly discovered I was just another grunt on an assignment. The company knew full well my potential, and they were going to use me to do the dirtiest work there was. My job was to work in a warehouse without air conditioning loading tires onto trucks.

Sometimes, to make things even hotter, they sent me to a place called "the hole." I had to climb up a long conveyer line, where I disappeared into a small opening. Way up there was a dimly lit area stacked with old tires. My assignment was to load the tires on to the conveyer belt and send them down to be loaded on trucks. Except for a brief lunch, I spent eight hours on my first day in that hole with no one to talk to except the occasional "hurry up." At the end of the day, I emerged from the hole with my cleanest, newest clothes covered in black sweat and grime. My body was painfully sore, and I was exhausted beyond belief.

But I was older now; it was the spring of 1985, and I was in Dallas where I wanted to be. I didn't care what the job was. I was finally making money. Every job, no matter what the assignment, I looked at as a possible opportunity to be successful.

I had a chance again to start anew and build a life. And it started on this day with this job, and it was within me. With each day, I worked hard to do the best job I could. I tried my best to leave a memorable impression with every customer, with my bosses, and with my co-workers. My job consisted of loading lumber and supplies on commercial trucks and into retail customer vehicles. I tried to learn everything I could about the lumber business as quickly as I could. As soon as I started to get the hang of the business, it changed. It wasn't just change like businesses go through every day. I mean the type of change that comes with a buyout. Lowe's Home Improvement purchased Boise Cascade. While others were nervous about their futures, the buyout in my mind increased the number of chances for me to make a difference.

On Track

My personal life was also starting to get on track. Julie and I were doing great; I was feeling accepted by her parents, and her friends liked me as well. My car was running good. It didn't take long before I got an apartment close to work and I even got a kitten (only to eventually have the apartment manager almost kick me out over it). I said good-bye to my friends Butch and Lana and would not see them again for several years.

Things really started to take off at my job, and I was promoted to receiving manager. Every day I would I do my best at my job. I tried to exert a little more energy and put more heart into my work. Since Lowe's had taken over, the store was being renovated and expanded. We were no longer just a lumberyard; we turned into a superstore, selling everything from appliances to furniture. This was just the type of challenge I needed to focus my newfound commitment and energy.

One day, we had received a truckload of appliances and I was the first one up on the truck; I began to drag the appliances to the edge of the truck as a forklift pulled up to unload them. I grabbed a large box containing a refrigerator and started to drag it toward the forklift when the box gave way, causing me to lose my grip. I fell from the back of the truck into the rising blades of the forklift. The driver screamed in fear. When I landed, one of the blades of the forklift had impaled my arm, and the fender of the forklift had gone through my knee. For a moment, I looked like a scarecrow hanging from the forklift. It took about forty stitches to repair the damage. I considered myself extremely lucky, considering how close I came to having to other parts of my body impaled. I was determined to succeed for once.

A day later, stitches and all, I was back to work giving it all I had. I worked twelve-hour days on a regular basis and if I didn't know how to do something, that wouldn't stop me. I would learn it. I was always trying to go the extra mile for the customer or trying to impress my bosses with my performance. I remember how that backfired on me too. One day we had a group of district and regional managers visit our store to see how the expansion construction was coming along. They were taking a tour with my bosses, the warehouse manager, and the operations managers. My boss stopped by where I was working in the lumberyard and introduced the group to me when suddenly out of the corner of my eye, I noticed a customer in need of assistance. I cut the introductions short with, "Excuse me. I see a customer in need of assistance." And with the grace of a gazelle, I ran across the yard. As I ran toward the customer, I could feel the Lowe's management team watching me and imagined them saying, "That young man is going to go somewhere in this business. Yes, he looks like management material to me."

Oh yes, I was feeling really good about myself. I approached the customer's vehicle in full stride. I planned to leap a small stack of timbers, but I caught my foot on the top one and went airborne across the parking lot. I rolled several times on the concrete, and I finally came to a stop right at the edge of the customer's car. The customer came to see if I was all right, just like the other managers who were watching my performance. I got up quickly saying, "I'm all right." The managers ended up loading the customer's car as I limped away, trying to wipe off the skid marks that covered my body. But I couldn't wipe off the red glow of embarrassment that covered my face. Cooley coordination and luck all at the same time.

Despite my lack of coordination, all of them knew my heart was into making the company successful and eventually I was promoted to assistant warehouse manager. I now had two managers and a team of twenty-six employees who reported to me. And it's a good thing my heart was into it, because the store was now deep into the construction and our warehouse manager quit. Lowe's brought in one of their warehouse managers, who was an expansion specialist. He may have had the experience with expansion, but he lacked experience working with people. I had some real problems with the way he treated some of the employees, and we had some intense differences of opinion.

I had been with Lowe's for just over a year and half when we were done with the construction. It was October 1986, and we were ready for the grand opening. We had all the fanfare of a gala event. We had balloons, free gift giveaways, stars like racecar driver Richard Petty and soccer star Tatu from the Dallas Sidekicks. It was a big deal, and it felt really good to know that all of the hard work was going to be the beginning of something big. Robert, my warehouse manager, told me that he would be moving on to another expansion, and I was going to be taking over the yard probably after the first of the year.

I was so excited about the prospect and with every job opening we had, I tried to recruit the very best employees. I even recruited people I knew away from their jobs because I knew what excellent workers they were. I was going to create the best team Lowe's had ever had.

I remember December 17, 1986, vividly. It was the day I learned a hard lesson about business management. We had heard the rumors that Lowe's was closing several of their stores in Texas, but we felt ours was safe. After all, our store was the only one that they had spent over a million dollars to expand. I showed up to work that day to see a group of employees outside the fence. I got out of my car and asked, "What's going on?"

An employee said, "You tell us! The fence is locked, and some guy in a suit said we should wait here." I tried my key to open the gate, and it would not work. So there we sat, waiting in the cold for answers. It was almost two hours later when a team of managers in suits came and opened the gate. As we walked to the front of the new store, the windows were covered in black poly-plastic. It was as if there has been a death, and in fact there was. It was the death of a store and the end of promising careers for some.

As we entered the store, they gathered us around one of the new registers, and then the district manager began to speak. In a straight, hard-as-stone face, he told us that they were going to close the store and everyone who had been there longer than a year would receive a severance package. For the others, they could help themselves to a Christmas tree on their way out. I stood in shock at what I was witnessing. How could a company underestimate the economy so much that they would spend all this money only to shut the store down?

I came back to reality as one of the girls that I had recruited from her job of three years came to me in tears, looked at me and asked, "Why?" I was crushed, hurt, and mad. Robert pulled me to the side and said, "Here's your severance pay. But I want you to know, I'd like you to come and work at one of the stores I go to next. I believe it's going to be in Arkansas."

"No thanks. I think I'll pass." Discouraged and disheartened, I walked out with a month's severance pay and out of a job, again.

Chapter 12:

On a Mission

Old proverb: "If at first you don't succeed, try, try again."

Instead of giving up and going back to my old ways, I was on a mission. It wasn't going to be easy. The economy was in a recession and jobs were scarce—and I don't just mean good jobs I mean *any* job. I was going to make it! So I searched the want ads and hit the pavement. I treated job hunting like it was a job. I was up at 8:00 a.m., reviewing newspapers and mapping out the places where I was going to apply. I would be out all day applying for jobs and sometimes interviewing. In less than two weeks, I had my next job offer. I was able to make my apartment payments, and Julie stuck by me.

I accepted a job as a shift leader for a preservatives plant. It was a division of Southland Corporation located in Oak Cliff, Texas. The plant wasn't located in exactly the safest part of the city. Just south of Dallas, Oak Cliff could be downright dangerous after dark, and I was lucky enough to pull third shift duty from 11:00 p.m. to 7:00 a.m. I knew I had to pay my dues, so I was there every evening at the start of my shift and worked as much overtime as they needed— and there was a lot of overtime.

I tried to learn everything I could about the preservatives business. I made huge batches of preservatives mixes, I worked with the laboratory technicians testing the preservatives, and I tried to learn as much as I could from those around me. I worked in an interesting part of town with an interesting crew. I was Caucasian, and every one of my team members was either Hispanic or African American. Not unlike me, most of them had a questionable past. All had arrest records, some for robbery, assault, and drugs, and one guy was a deserter from the Army. I don't think this crew was too thrilled with the fact that "some white boy" was hired to tell them what to do. But that wasn't my purpose at all.

> I just wanted to get on my feet, and I knew that the only way I was going to do that was to give this job all I could.

So I did. I stayed late, I came in early, and I participated in every program the company offered and made suggestions to improve quality. I tried to make my team the most productive, quality-conscious group in the company.

Team Troubles

It wasn't easy to gain the support of the team I inherited. They didn't want much to do with me and sure didn't want to follow orders, especially one individual named Lawrence Lamb. Lawrence was a black guy who stood about six-foot-five and weighed about 280 pounds. From the start, he didn't seem to care for me and would try to manipulate the team to revolt against me. I was told that one of the reasons the last shift leader left the company was because of Lawrence. Apparently, Lawrence lost his temper one night and took it out on the shift leader. From what I heard, Lawrence grabbed a 40-pound pallet with one hand and threw it at the shift leader's head. The shift leader was so shaken by the incident that he quit.

Lawrence did his best to start trouble wherever and whenever he could. He would talk negatively about the company, talk negatively to his peers, and almost every time I passed by, he would have a negative comment to make to me. Still, I needed to either work with this guy or get rid of him. And as a brand new shift leader, I didn't have much clout to be firing someone. I decided to try to find a way to work with him. I learned about his past and eventually learned what motivated him. He had been with Southland for about five years and prior to that, he had been in prison for assault and battery. Lawrence almost killed someone and had to serve some time in prison. I also found out that Lawrence was motivated by money. He worked two other jobs aside from working at Southland on third shift. He was very reliable, always showing up on time and if it didn't conflict with his other jobs, he would work overtime whenever needed. That and the fact that he intimidated some of the managers helped him to retain his job so long. Getting to know my team was one of the smartest things I had done.

One night, an employee said that I better do something quick because Lawrence was getting ready to kill Nathan in the batch room. The batch room was a huge room made of concrete with thirty-foot ceilings and two twenty-foot-tall mixing tanks. The room was big enough to maneuver a forklift in and out. It reminded me of a mad scientist's laboratory from some B-movie. I ran down the ramp to the room to see Lawrence and Nathan in a standoff. The only thing that was saving Nathan was the point of a razorblade knife that he was swinging at Lawrence. Just as I got to the bottom of the ramp, Lawrence was getting ready to lunge at Nathan. Before he did, I grabbed Lawrence around his huge frame of a body—probably not one of the smartest things I had ever done, but if I didn't, I felt someone would be seriously hurt. As I looked over at Nathan, I could see the fear in his eyes, but I knew that he would have used the knife. When I grabbed Lawrence, his head turned toward me and I could see the rage in his eyes—a rage that I had seen in my own eyes before. "Are you out of your mind?"

I looked him square in the eyes and said, "If you do this, you will be fired, and you will lose a large amount of money. Let it go." About that time, I could feel the tension in his body start to subside and he relaxed. Just then, another shift leader came running down the ramp and flew into both of us, driving us backwards into the forklift.

The guy yelled, "Lawrence, don't do it! It's not worth it!"

He thought that Lawrence was trying to kill me because everyone knew how much Lawrence disliked me. Both Lawrence and I kind of laughed about it and told him he could let go. The reason for the fight was petty—Lawrence felt disrespected by Nathan and snapped. Not unlike a lot of the reasoning that I used to see in jail between inmates. The next day, Lawrence was put on an internal counseling program sponsored by the company.

While at Southland, I also made a good friend that would last long after my tenure with Southland was over. Jimmy joined Southland about the same time I did, and he had the same position but he worked on a different shift. Jimmy was a black guy that was a little older than I was, but from the start we had a lot in common. We were both aggressive and wanted to do what we could to be successful, and it was getting noticed by the management. Jimmy and I also started hanging out socially on the weekends or whenever we had the same days off. We would party. Here was another guy who transcended the color barriers.

Jimmy could go to a cowboy bar as easily as he could a black bar, and we did both. However, the black clubs in Dallas were a lot different from the underground black shanty bars of Gainesville, Texas. Some of these clubs were fantastic, like Fat Sollys in South Dallas. One night, Jimmy and I walked through the door. The place was huge! There were several bars within the bar. On one side, they had a jazz bar with the sound of a saxophone playing in the background. Upstairs, they had slow music playing and downstairs they had hip-hop, which was really gaining popularity in the late '80s. There were several hundred people in the bar, yet I was the only white guy. Jimmy would tell me that they probably thought I was crazy, so that's why I didn't get in any trouble. And I guess all the other black bars we went to thought I was crazy as much as the cowboy bars must have felt Jimmy was crazy for showing up there. Where have I heard this before?

The truth was we just didn't let color limit us and if we felt like hanging out somewhere different, we did. I learned a whole lot about good jazz music from hanging out in some of the black clubs.

> Yeah, we still drank quite a bit, but I was working to rise from the ashes like a Phoenix. Work was really my addiction now.

Healthy Competition

Back at work, Jimmy and I also had another common interest. We both wanted the same promotion to production supervisor. While we were both somewhat competitive, we were both also very supportive of each other. Our goal and our teamwork turned out big results for the company. Productivity was up and rework was down. And when all was said and done, management made their decision. We were both promoted; Jimmy was promoted over a different department, and I was promoted over our department.

One day after my shift, I went to my truck and it wouldn't start. I was working with a self-proclaimed mechanic and while I was priming the carburetor with gasoline, the guy jumped into the car and tried to start it. The truck backfired and shot gasoline and fire right up my shirtsleeve. I jumped from underneath the hood of the truck as my shirt was going up in flames. I tried to put the flame out, but the gas made it impossible. I could feel my face burning; my hair was on fire, and the shirt was melting the skin on my arms and body. Out of nowhere, Jimmy barreled across the parking lot and without a second thought he ripped the shirt from my body and threw the flaming piece of cloth to the side. Then, he became my ambulance and rushed me to the hospital where third-degree burns were replaced with skin grafts.

The next day, I was back to work with bandages up my arm and around my body. I was ready to pick up where I left off on my training. I lived for work and wanted to continue to get ahead. Unfortunately, our training would be short-lived. It was October 1988; the plant had been sold and everyone in the plant would be losing his or her job in about thirty days.

I thought to myself, *Not again, what have I done to deserve this punishment?* I had worked *so* hard! I was trying to clean up my life. Without warning, I was kicked back down to being without a job—again. My self-esteem and financial status was shaky at best. I didn't know how I would handle yet another setback. Where do I go now?

Looking Back

This was the turning point in my life; I had survived what I believed was as bad as it could get and in the process, I had grown. I had to make some better choices thus, making some changes. I was smart enough to see where I was heading, and it was a *dead* end. Fortunately, I was also mature enough but still young enough to change and to learn from my bad choices to move on. From failed relationships to losing jobs, it just didn't seem I was meant to be successful at anything. At the time, I often thought it would be so easy just to give up and succumb to all the temptations that were pulling me down. However, if temptations and failed attempts were pulling me down, a whole new set of opportunities were getting ready to lift me up, and this time I was not going to backslide.

SECTION 4:
ADULT YEARS

Chapter 13:

Starting Over—Again

Southland did a really good thing. They worked with their top people and lined up interviews at other companies. Even better than that, they had the companies come to Southland to interview us. So while we worked through the day, we could go to interviews at the plant. I also kept an eye on the classifieds and set up an interview or two on my own. I came across a small ad for a shipping assistant. Once again, I was willing to do almost anything to pay my rent; I thought I would apply. Another reason I applied for a lesser position with lesser pay is that after losing two jobs, any confidence I had gained had vanished. I sent my resume to the company and got an interview.

The ActionSystems directions led me to an absolutely beautiful building in the middle of North Dallas County. I entered the revolving doors into a beautiful marble interior. It was like nothing I had ever seen before. And as I rode up the rosewood and mirror-lined elevator to the fourteenth floor, all I could think of was that this place would never give me a job in my *Miami Vice* tie and my polyester pants from Wal-Mart. When the doors to the elevator opened, I had a whole new thought—turn around and run! This was the classiest place I had ever even been in, much less considered working for. I held it together while telling the receptionist I was there for an interview. As I waited, I remember talking myself into staying by saying, *It's only a shipping assistant's job. I can do this.*

When Mike Carcasole showed up in the lobby, I was as ready to interview as I was going to get. Mike and I seemed to bond instantly, and when he was done asking his questions and I answered them to the best of my ability, he told me they would get back to me. I went away feeling pretty good about my chances.

About the same time, I got a call from one of the interviews that was conducted through Southland. I was offered a job as a shift leader for Oak Farm Dairies. I accepted the job; after all, it was as good as what I had been doing at Southland with a little better money. I started to work at Oak Farms on second shift and even though I was only off for a couple of weeks, I was glad to be back to work.

ActionSystems called me back in for another interview. Since I was working nights, I could make the interview. I already had a job, but something besides my truck drove me to that interview. When I returned, I interviewed with the production manager (Mike's boss) and as with Mike, the interview went really well. Afterwards, Mike gave me a tour of the company. As we walked down the halls, he introduced me to many of the business professionals. I was really impressed with the people and even more impressed with the over-all culture there. After the interview and the tour, I went to work at Oak Farms, but I couldn't stop thinking about ActionSystems.

I'd been with Oak Farms for a week, and I was struggling with the job. The position did not seem like it fit me. The daily routine was monotonous. I was not relating to the employees well. Many would spend their breaks out at their cars, and from the looks of their eyes when they returned, they were using mind-altering substances and drinking booze during break. This was something I was trying to get away from now; as was the case with Talanya's, that element was a part of my job.

ActionSystems made me an offer, but it was lower than I was making and the position was yet another step back from Oak Farms.

Still, there was something about the place. I told Mike I would consider the offer and get back to him. That evening, I went back to Oak Farms. I really evaluated my future if I stayed at Oak Farms and decided I was not going to be a fit and they would probably find someone that was better suited for the company. The next day, I turned in my notice and fortunately, my boss let me off the hook. I called Mike back and accepted his offer.

> I was prepared to find out about the feeling that was guiding me to be a part of this company.

I officially started at ActionSystems on December 12, 1988 and from the very first day, my feelings did nothing but grow. There was something about this company that made it a fit for me.

One of the other things I was attracted to early on was the challenge. In my very first month, there would be many. That beautiful office turned out to be just a place for me to visit. My work location actually turned out to be a couple of blocks away in a warehouse. This is where I would be stationed with my supervisor, Mike. The warehouse was just a shell, and it was Mike's job to turn it into a productive distribution center. My job was to assist in whatever capacity he needed. Behind the scenes, I created the plans for the layout of the distribution center, coordinated the movement of all inventory from the corporate office to the distribution center, set up the inventory, and set up some of the processes for shipping and receiving our training materials. While Mike was happy to assist, he spent a lot of his time complaining about how he wasn't being treated fairly. Less than a month later, ActionSystems held the grand opening of their distribution center. All the corporate executives were there. I stood behind Mike as he was praised by the owner, Robert Hall, for his hard work in setting up a productive distribution center. Robert and ActionSystems were really good at praising people for their contributions. They did it up right, a ribbon-cutting ceremony, a champagne toast and yes...food!

After the hoopla, all the employees went back to the office, leaving Mike and me to start being productive. As the days went by, Mike continued to be more frustrated with what he classified as unfair treatment and low pay. In the meantime, we had product to ship. So while Mike spent his time voicing his complaints and looking for a job, I was doing my best to figure out what the heck I was supposed to be doing. I was actually enjoying this work. I had flexibility, empowerment to manage myself, and I saw opportunity but I wasn't in a hurry.

Things are Looking Up

In my personal life, I was still with Julie and after being together for three years, we were finally going to get a place together. We ended up getting a small apartment, but it was closer to work and I was feeling good. I told Julie that I know my job wasn't much, but I could see some real potential for the future. I wasn't going to be so aggressive on trying to get ahead and would just focus on learning my job. I also wanted her to know that I planned to focus on building a stronger relationship. After all, we were now living together, and I knew it was important to her. Meanwhile Julie was busy focusing on her education and a job of her own. So even though we didn't have a lot of money, life was starting to shape up for us.

Mike's frustration with ActionSystems had reached a boiling point. He went to his boss, Steve, and told him about his discontent and that he was going to start looking for another job unless he was recognized appropriately and received an increase in salary. Mike thought that Steve would realize that the company couldn't survive without his services and would give him a big fat raise. Steve listened but did not agree to do anything, which only increased Mike's frustration. In the meantime, I was working with some temporaries and putting together a pretty effective operation. In the days to come, Mike came in less and less and when he did, he'd be full of bitterness about the company. But his bitterness was nothing compared to the day he was looking through the classified section of the paper and saw that ActionSystems, an international consulting firm, was running an ad for a Material Control Supervisor, which coincidentally was Mike's title. Mike was furious and hurt. He was going to quit and when he did, he was going to make sure the entire management knew it. So, when the managers went to lunch, he put his resignation letter on each one of their chairs; I guess he showed them.

Mike was gone, and they were interviewing for his replacement. Meanwhile, I was keeping the place running, but no one on the management team really knew who I was. I took a chance and replied to the ad, sending my resume in for the supervisor position. They had already interviewed several candidates when I was finally interviewed. I must have made an impression because it was down to three candidates—me and two other guys. They called me for another interview and in less than two months after I started at ActionSystems, I was promoted. I also got a good increase from my previous starting annual salary of $16,900. With the promotion also came the overtime. I was on a mission to make the position and the company all it could be.

At home, Julie was also spending a lot of time at work, school, and studying. We had a little more money, so we moved into a bigger place. You would think that things would get better; instead there was more tension. We started to argue, which is something we had never really done before. I started to think that this relationship was getting too serious, and it was scaring me. I began to feel the pressure of trying to provide a life for her like she had at home with her parents. I was trying to do it all—trying to make better money, to give her everything I felt she deserved, to be there for her, and to protect her. I had always thought she was better than I deserved, and I basically pressured myself out of the relationship. Instead of being with her more, I started to be with her less. I worked later and I showed her less attention when I was home. She never did anything to deserve it, but one day I sat down with her and told her I wanted her to move back home. I told her I couldn't provide her with the life she deserved and she needed to move back home, where she could focus on her degree and not have to worry about bills. I guess all of the pressure had gotten to me, and she was the victim.

Throughout our relationship, Julie was a calm, rational, soft-spoken woman. As I delivered this news, she listened intently and when I was finished, she snapped and attacked me! She beat me on every one of my body parts and when she was done she left. A few days later, she packed her things and left for good. I drove away the only really good woman that I felt ever loved me in my entire life. While it hurt me in a way I will never forget, I wasn't about to let my pain show. Instead, I tried to hide my pain by returning to my old ways—partying and alcohol. I also started working out. Instead of exercising for health reasons, I did it to cover up my insecurity and lack of confidence. I was in my late '20s now and was starting to notice when I went out, that I wasn't as young as the others in the nightclubs. I was trying to do something to slow down Father Time, or is it Mother Nature?

Joe Athlete

Most of the people that frequented the athletic club were older men and younger women. I felt good that there wasn't any competition for the women, and then I noticed this guy coming into the gym. I remember sizing him up, thinking, *Who does this guy think he is?* He looked like he just got here from the California surf. He had long blonde hair, was tanned, and well built. My candy store was being invaded. Every time I would see him, I would make a habit if giving him the "look." (You know the one, the look that says you ain't anything.) The funny thing was he would give me the same look back. For weeks, we worked out at the same time and avoided saying anything to each other, as we both would separately try to talk to the same girls at the gym.

One day, I noticed a really nerdy looking guy make his way into the work out area. This guy looked like skinny Jerry Lewis as he walked up to the machine. Wearing his black-framed glasses, he grabbed the handles of the lat pull down machine, took a deep breath and started to pull with all his might. It was then that I saw that there was no weight on the cable. When he pulled those handles, it was like someone had pulled a chair out from underneath this guy and he flew to the floor but he didn't let go of the handles. He looked like a puppet bouncing up and down and spinning all around. About that time, the guy who had been my competition and I looked at each other and busted out laughing. When the puppet finally got control, he turned to see if anyone saw his performance. We grabbed our weights and pretended not to have noticed. He quickly left, and we died laughing again. My competition turned out to be a guy named Chris. We've been friends ever since.

Chris was different from other guys I had run around with. Sure, we both had women on the brain and would go to all the nightspots to meet them. But it didn't take long before I realized this guy was something different. When we went out he hardly drank, he never did drugs, and I never have seen anyone as picky when it came to women. Chris also had some great hobbies. One was playing the guitar, and he was pretty good. He was a big fan of a heavy metal guitar. His other hobby was painting, and he was an excellent artist. I also had a similar hobby in drawing, so we had other things to talk about besides just women. Chris was, for the most part, a good influence on me.

We got in the habit of going out almost every weekend and the nightclubs got to know us well. It was thanks to Chris that my drinking actually started to decrease.

> For the first time in my life, I realized that I could go out and have a good time without being high or drunk.

I also liked remembering the next day what I had done the night before. I learned a lot about being a better person thanks to Chris. He had a uncanny way of making you feel like what was going on in your life was more important than what he had going on—when in reality he led a most interesting life.

By night, sometimes we would party, but it wouldn't be unusual for Chris to stay home and play his guitar or work on a painting. By day, Chris was a graphic designer working for some of the best advertising firms in Dallas. He graduated from the University of Arizona with a degree in graphic design. Graduating from college was something we did not have in common.

Despite splitting up with Julie, life wasn't too bad. My job was good, and I was making new friends but still something was missing—there was a void in my life. I would often think about Julie and try to tell myself, "You couldn't have married her. What would people think? After all, her married name would have been "Julie Cooley."

In previous situations, it was usually about this time I would turn back to getting in trouble with partying and alcohol. This time, I decided to fill the void with something different. I was determined to go back to school and get a degree. Cooley the college boy. I kinda liked the sound of that.

Chapter 14:

Back To School

Aside from getting my GED in 1984, I had not been to school since 1979, and that didn't really count. It was now 1989, and at twenty-seven, I was walking into a college for the first time.

One day on my way home, I had stopped by a small college about a mile from work. I didn't have a clue where to start. I knew I wanted to do better in my job. I wanted to get into management and eventually I would like to own my own business. Somehow, I found a collection of courses devoted to a career in "mid-management"; that sounded like as good a place as any to start. But it wasn't going to be easy. It had been so long since I'd been in school. I had to take a series of tests to determine how many prerequisite courses I needed before I could start taking mid-management classes.

By the "skin of my teeth," I passed the tests in reading, English, and the dreaded math. That was the first obstacle; I could not afford (both time and cash were against me) to take a lot of prerequisite courses. Also, I was afraid that if I had to take the basic courses again I would have become disinterested, like in high school.

During the day, I worked until about 6:00 p.m., then I rushed to class which lasted until almost 10:00 p.m. It made for a long day, but it kept me off the streets. I was really surprised to find that there were a lot of students in my age group. I started doing pretty well in my management classes and also developed a great relationship with the management instructor, Gene Hilton. I guess he noticed something in me, or maybe he made all of his students feel this way. He was a source of constant encouragement. He challenged me to do more than just his class. Before I knew it, I was volunteering for campus clubs, and I became part of a campus group called AMS (Administrative Management Society).

My life was officially filled up. I was working sixty hours a week, taking two classes a semester, exercising, hanging out with Chris, and getting back into dating again. Being in college also allowed me to meet people of a whole different breed. A lot of them were just like me (okay, maybe not quite the same background)—they had spent years either down on their luck, raising a family, or trying to better themselves in their career. I started dating some girls from the college and of course the one I got hooked on was probably the last person I should have been with.

She showed up to class one day, and I could not take my eyes off of her. She looked like a model that just walked out of a French design magazine. I was really bad when it came to striking up a conversation, but she wasn't. Before I had time to stumble all over my words, she let me off the hook and made it easy for me. Her name was Danielle and almost from the introduction we became room-mates—at my apartment of course. Danielle turned out to actually be a model, albeit part-time for some department store catalogs. She also liked to party, and she used her looks to use men.

Danielle didn't know that I had been down that road before, and I wasn't going there again. For a little while, I thought I could save Danielle from her future.

For whatever reason, I always thought I should try to save other people when I couldn't even save myself.

The only thing I would end up doing is getting myself in deeper and deeper. I started out trying to save Danielle from her past of being neglected by her mother and ending up in an orphanage. I ended up switching gears to try to help her sister out of an abusive relationship with her husband. It got so complicated that I moved her sister and her child back to Dallas to stay with us. So there I was with Danielle, her sister, and her sister's child, all living in a one-bedroom apartment that I could barely afford. Four weeks later, Danielle went back into a relationship with a guy who owned a designer apparel store. Her sister stayed with me and eventually moved out to get a place of her own.

I continued to give it my all and excel at work and in school. I completed all of my management courses, became certified in mid-management, and was carrying a 4.0 GPA. I was also the President of the Brookhaven College Chapter of the American Management Society (AMS). I was coming out of my shell and before I knew it, the young guy that only a few years ago couldn't speak to one person was speaking to groups of sixty people. In AMS, we were putting together one of the largest memberships that Gene had seen at the college.

> At work I was receiving more promotions, and it wasn't because I was the smartest or the most educated—it was because I was committed to making the company successful. I gave whatever it took.

I tried to work a little bit harder than the next person and added value with problem solving suggestions. I didn't understand the words "impossible" or "quit." I just made it happen, and I would take on every challenge that came my way. Maybe my solutions were not always the best or the smartest, but they got the problem solved. I felt I was on fire, and I was energized by the reward of success.

Banking Industry Bust

From 1987 until 1989, we had grown from around fifteen people to over a hundred. With the new decade came the fall of the banking industry. There were many bank foreclosures, executives going to jail, banks closing, and the merger wars were on. The volatile environment took its toll on us. Sound familiar? We had just gone through another downturn, and banking was involved again. But this was the early '90s. We had been growing to meet our customers' demand and when the bottom fell out, suddenly we had no customers.

It was a dark day on the Friday before Columbus Day, 1990, when all the employees were called together in our conference room. When we gathered, some were missing. Robert and his management team had worked the last three months without a salary, and now he had to make an even harder decision. That is when I watched Robert do the most difficult thing an owner of a company must do. He stood before the group with tear-filled eyes and told of how the marketplace had taken its toll on our company. He turned the pages on a flipchart to reveal the names of employees that had been let go. He tried to hold back the tears as he went down the list, but the pain was too much.

I was thinking to myself, *what is this?* This is so different from what I had seen with any job I had ever been with. None had ever showed such emotion about a layoff. I realized this owner actually cared about each and every person. Robert understood that these people have families, which meant more than a company that was losing money. Even though Robert probably didn't know half the people he had just laid off personally, he cared for them as individuals. I had less seniority than many of the employees at ActionSystems, so I waited to hear my name, but it was never called. That was the moment I committed myself to do whatever I could to make Robert's company a success. His leadership style, his personal values, and his concern for his employees made a lasting impression on me. I would do whatever I could to ensure that Robert would never have to stand before his employees and tell them that their friends were no longer a part of the organization.

I survived the layoff, and I guess I will never know why I was spared. Was it because my salary wasn't big enough for them to worry about or was it because I added value that would be hard to replace? I choose to believe the latter, but of course so did the other Mike, and we know what that got him. The layoffs would continue and one by one, jobs were being eliminated. Someone had to pick up the responsibilities, and I volunteered for all that I could. On one hand, I felt I had everything before me; yet, on the other hand, I was as lost as I had ever been. Everything I was accomplishing was to no avail if I had no one to share it with.

Chris and I continued to go to the nightclubs. We had VIP entrance into most of them, and many people knew who we were. We would hook up with friends, meet girls, and drink. A lot of times, these nights just led to trouble—whether it be a fight or a broken heart. To us, women were a conquest, a bet. One of our unwritten rules was not to get too close and never get attached. Whenever this happened we would break it off. We were living a good life. We could afford nice cars and a nice place to live. Eventually, we decided to become roommates, and we set our sights on the dream bachelor pad. We leased an incredible condominium overlooking a great pool and Jacuzzi. On the surface, we appeared to have it all, but I still felt lost and that something was missing.

Chapter 15:

A New Chapter In Life

Chris had been a friend to this girl for quite sometime, but then he started dating her. One night, she asked him if he had a buddy for her friend. She said she wanted this guy to be nice, because her friend was trying to get out of a difficult relationship and she needed someone to help her move on. To this day, I don't know why Chris recommended me.

> Given my past history, I had the potential to be the worst person she had ever dated.

Although I didn't know it, God was watching over us. I took a chance. I will never forget the night I was introduced to Lisa. It was New Year's Eve, 1991, and she was working as a coat check girl at one of the clubs that Chris and I frequented. I thought to myself, *Okay, she is hot, but this girl doesn't have much of a future if her career goals are to be a coat check girl at a nightclub*. She was sure beautiful with her slender five-foot-seven frame and her long and fiery red hair.

I'm not very good at starting a conversation, but there was an instant connection with Lisa. She was so shy that no matter what I said sounded good. Her smile captivated me instantly and the fact that she laughed at my sense of humor was all the encouragement I needed—I was hooked. Still, I thought she would be good for a few laughs and maybe a couple of dates and then I would move on. Because I didn't know where I was going, I sure didn't want to commit to another person who didn't know where she was going.

Don't Judge a Book By Its Cover

As Lisa and I went out a few times, I found myself surprisingly more attracted to her than I thought I would be. I found myself watching the clock, knowing I was going to go see her. Over time, I learned that this lady had more goals than most people. I had initially made a grand misjudgment of her. I am so glad I listened to my heart on this one. I thought Lisa's life goal was to be a "coat check girl." She only did that on weekend nights. During the weekdays, she went to school full-time at Texas Women's University, where her major was nutrition. She also worked part-time as a waitress and part-time as a caterer. In her spare time, she exercised and her athletic build made that obvious. So let's see, she likes to work out and I like to work out. I wanted to eat better, and she was studying to be a nutritionist. She worked hard to get what she wanted, and I worked hard to get what I wanted. I would have to say we had some things in common. Maybe too much in common, I wasn't sure what "it" was, but "it" was getting kinda scary.

Oh no, here we go again. What was I thinking? Did I forget how many times I had been hurt by women that I had tried to love? I kept trying to drive her away, but in my heart I knew that she was the one. (Lisa would later tell me that she knew I was the one from "day one," and she was not going to give up on me.)

Back at the job, I was working a ton of hours, and I was forcing myself to hang out with the guys, even though I would have much rather have been with Lisa. I just wasn't going to get caught in that trap again. Lisa was understandably confused, but she gave me my space and it wasn't hard because she was a busy person as well. This on-again, off-again dating went on for about a year while we also dated other people.

Lisa moved from her apartment back home with her parents who lived in an affluent part of the Dallas/Fort Worth area. I really got to know her family and for the most part, they were a close family with many relatives living in Nevada. Her dad and I actually got along, and I later found out that was a double bonus because it's the first time I can recall that I got along with any girl's parents. Lisa told me that her dad had never liked any of her boyfriends.

Despite our different backgrounds, there were a lot of similarities between her father and me. Her dad's name was Al, and he was raised in a low-income family and grew up doing anything he could to make ends meet. He raised a family that included three children; he worked full-time and went to college to get an engineering degree. He had long since received his degree, and was a quality assurance engineer in the electronics industry.

Her mother was an executive assistant and was probably smarter than most of the executives she supported. She sacrificed her career goals to raise a family. She doesn't see it as a sacrifice at all.

Physically, you couldn't tell that Lisa's two brothers were related. Her older brother, Joe, was blonde, introverted, and was a hard worker dedicated to whatever job he worked, but I don't believe he thought he was cut out for college. He had been with the same girl for some time and had what seemed to be a very dependent personality. Dave, the youngest, had brown hair and was more extroverted; he knew and hung out with a lot of people, went to college and seemed to take everything in stride, including his dating life.

Collectively, they were the most "normal" family I had met. I enjoyed spending time with them (and Lisa, too, of course!). I had a new perspective on "family," and it was a good one. I didn't know it at the time, but the goodness and godliness I had experienced with Lisa's family planted a seed of hope in me for a better life.

An Extreme Endeavor

Chris and I got together, and in addition to our full-time jobs, we created a graphics design company that we called Extreme Design.

Chris's role was using his unique style of art to create something different in the marketplace. My job was to increase sales and manage the business. And increase sales we did—in fact, it didn't take long before we had to make a decision about whether we should think about leaving our full-time jobs and dedicate ourselves fully to Extreme Design.

We had a strong client base, and the business was growing. It was also taking more and more of our time. What made Chris good was his ability to use his creativity, and what made me good was my ability to be disciplined (and after my past, that was hard to believe). Too often, our two different personalities would clash. I would overcommit to our customers, and Chris would under-deliver, thus leaving some of our clients out to dry. After our first year, we had earned almost $20,000 part-time, but that would be our only year in business as we realized that we wouldn't make the best of business partners, but we still stayed the best of friends.

At ActionSystems, we were running very lean—the company that was once over a hundred had now dipped below twenty employees. The number of jobs I was doing and the amount of hours I was putting in was almost unbearable. One night Robert, another executive, and I were working until 1:00 a.m., trying to complete a project. We needed to deliver it to a customer, so we could invoice them and make our payroll. Things got so bad that Robert asked his wife to come in and help manage parts of the company. Linda was going to take over the management of several departments. One of those departments was mine. I recall thinking, *This is just what I need, reporting to the boss's wife! I bet she is some piece of work. She probably doesn't know anything about managing a company!* Once again, I would be proven wrong.

To top it all off, I had serious challenges among some of my team members. They just couldn't work together. Two in particular were really having problems—so much so that they both ended up leaving the company. This was something that the rest of my team members didn't appreciate, and they let me know it by rebelling.

After the two employees left, I was doing both their jobs as well. It was December and we were approaching the end of our quarter, and things were still tight at ActionSystems. Again, there was doubt to whether we would make our payroll or not. So I focused my energy on shipping product and working over eighty hours a week. The last week of December was critical, so I shipped over $100,000 worth of product in one week to help get through the end of the year and past another quarter. During that time, not one of my six team members offered to help. Every afternoon, they would leave on time and were never early to work. This just wasn't like my team.

We Didn't Cover This in Management 101

One day, I was called into the conference room and there across the table sat my entire staff and Linda. As I sat down, Linda began to facilitate the meeting, and eventually the group started opening up and sharing how upset they were with me. They wondered how I could let those two team members leave. They started questioning my ability to communicate with them. They felt I was always questioning what they were doing instead of helping them and supporting them. Even the little things were affecting them like not wishing them a good morning. I sat on the other side of the table thinking, *How can this be happening? Do they not know what I've been doing behind the scenes so they would get a paycheck?*

I was hurt and defensive, and it was all I could do to keep from lashing out. When the team was done addressing the issues they had, I was crushed, and feeling betrayed and set up.

> I walked away thinking that my career was over; I would surely never be the same again. I was learning a valuable lesson, but at the time I didn't realize it.

For the next few months, I was lifeless going through the motions of my job. I was constantly questioning myself in everything I was doing. I was expecting to be fired any day. I had let my team down, I had let Robert down, and I had let the company down. Every intention I had backfired. The bottom line: I was feeling sorry for myself, and my work was getting off track.

One day, Robert pulled me into his office, and Linda was there, so I prepared myself for the inevitable. I just knew the next day I would be on the street again looking for a job. As I sat down at the conference table, I must have looked as useless an employee they had ever seen. Robert began to speak and told me that I was not performing at the level I was expected to perform. I responded to Robert and Linda with some lame excuses, and how I was still struggling with the team meeting that occurred a few months ago.

Robert listened and when I was done he leaned up to the table and blew me away when he said, "You know what, it's time you get over it. I need you out there performing. The company needs you out there making it happen. We need everyone giving it all they got to get ActionSystems back on top."

> That was the last thing I expected to hear, and it was just the "slap in the face" that I needed. From here on out, I'm going back to giving it my all.

I was re-energized toward our success but the late nights, the challenging client expectations, and the fact that we were so short-staffed started to take its toll. I don't know how Robert and Linda always knew just the right time to stop and listen, but they did. Robert was working as hard as anyone else. I was working one weekend to get another last minute project out when I received a call from Robert on his cell phone. He was running around taking his kids to different events, but he picked me up and took me riding around with him. In between dropping one kid off and picking up another, he listened as I vented and expressed my opinions of the state of the company. I had never felt so much a part of the company as I did on that day. His values and willingness to share his time with me made such a lasting impression. Also on that day, Robert became more than an owner, he made me a part of his family, and he made a friend for life.

Hard Work Pays Off

It was 1994, and the hard work started to pay off for ActionSystems. We started getting more business than we knew what to do with, and that brought on a whole new set of issues. We were now back in the growing mode and recruiting was critical. Linda Hall turned her attention here, and I was promoted to production manager. Action-Systems was on its way back to the top, and this time, we were only looking back to ensure we didn't make the same mistakes as before.

My relationship with Lisa continued to get stronger. She was an unbelievably caring person, so it was no surprise when she put her nutrition degree to use really helping others. She worked as a dietician for the state in a government-funded program. Her job was working with low-income families to provide nutrition programs and free food to help sustain a healthy diet for mothers, infants, and children. She was such an inspiration to me when I looked at what she did for a living. What she did went beyond just making a dollar. She wasn't paid what she could be if she had her own private practice, but with her, it wasn't about the money—it was about making a difference and helping others. She really helped me to take a hard look at my goals, my values, and my life, and make some choices and changes.

I was falling deeply in love. I wanted her to be my wife, but everything had to be just perfect. I started my search for the perfect ring; I put on my thinking cap to come up with just the right way to propose, and I even started searching for a house. Lisa knew none of this. I know that because she was making it clear she wasn't going to wait around forever. It was all I could do to hold my tongue, and I prayed she would be patient just a little longer. That special evening came in September 1994 when I took her to a romantic restaurant that incidentally used to be one of the homes of decorated World War II hero and actor Audie Murphy. I proposed to her over dessert (which is also where I hid the ring). We set a date for the wedding and bought a house. I couldn't believe it; I was going to be married again—but this time for the right reasons. Together, Lisa and I were going to buy our first home. God had given me several chances at life, and this time I was going to make it count!

Chapter 16:

Another Chance At Life

Lisa is Catholic. Before we could be married in the Catholic church, we were expected to go through a three-day program called Engaged Encounter. Now I didn't mind getting married in the Catholic church even though I was loosely called a Baptist, but to go through some program that was going to try to brainwash me wasn't in my plans. Still, I really loved Lisa and she was so deeply embedded in the tradition of her religion that if it was required, I would participate.

We arrived in Ft. Worth on a Friday to an old facility that belonged to the Catholic church. I was ready to endure three days of religion being shoved down my throat. Lisa and I walked into a large room with about fifteen other couples. As we took our seats, I looked around and noticed that there were about fifteen guys with same look on their faces thinking the same thing: *I cannot believe I have to be here.* Then in walked three couples. The lead couple sat on a couch positioned in the center of a small stage.

For the remainder of the weekend, those couples shared their personal testimonials about the challenges they have faced in their marriages. They focused not only on religion, but also communication, love, forgiveness, and even sex. I was moved by their willingness to open up to perfect strangers. These couples shared with conviction, heart, love, and compassion. It was not uncommon for the women and men to break down and cry. I was deeply moved by the experience of these three days. It was a great foundation for our marriage.

Lisa and I got married on October 14, 1995. My best man was Chris and my groomsmen were my brother, Marty, my good friends Kurtis, Jimmy, and Gregory. Our ushers were Lisa's two brothers, Dave and Joe. Yes, this was definitely a very diverse group of friends. Chris had rich parents, went to a private school, went to a major university on a full scholarship, and was an outstanding graphic artist. Kurtis went to a trade school and became a sheet metal worker, strong in the union. He was a family man with three kids. Jimmy was African American and went on to become a senior project manager for a telecommunications company. Gregory was much older than most of my friends, was an extremely intelligent man, highly educated, and was one of the senior consultants at ActionSystems. Nothing made me prouder than to hear Gregory speak to others and tell them that I was his best friend at ActionSystems. He helped to give me the confidence I needed to be successful. And as for my brother, he was married with three beautiful daughters, and had three successful car dealerships in the greater St. Louis area.

The only thing that was more beautiful than the day was my new wife. She was absolutely stunning, and it was the wedding I had always dreamed of, but always thought I was dreaming about someone else's perfect wedding. I was happier than I had ever been. The honeymoon was a wondrous adventure through Florida and a short cruise to the Bahamas. Everything was so great

> I thought I would wake up from this dream any moment, but I didn't. This dream is now my life.

I was so affected by the three days of our marriage encounter. Lisa and I were moved so much that we volunteered to participate in the Engaged Encounter program. For two years, we served as greeters, helped in the kitchen, and eventually moved to become a "couch couple." There I was in front of a bunch of strangers, sharing some of our own challenges in marriage. Inevitably before the weekend was done, even I was tearing up over the love of my wife. I realized we were actually helping people, and I wanted to continue. This may have been the first inkling of where God and my life would take me in later years.

Luck is a Lady

At home, I had a wonderful wife and a happy and healthy environment to keep me growing strong. At work, the company was on its way back and we were now short-staffed and everyone was taking on as many responsibilities as possible. As luck would have it, Linda turned out to be one of my best mentors. She, like Robert, cared about everyone and wanted to see everyone be successful. She taught me so much about dealing with the people side of the business. Behind the scenes, she was unselfishly giving me credit for things that would otherwise go unnoticed. She taught me so much about how to be the type of leader that I wanted to be. Linda absolutely brought out the best in me. I was in an environment with good values and good role models.

The day Linda told me she had breast cancer I flipped out. Linda handled it better than I did. She went through surgery and started radiation treatments, yet she continued to do her job. She handled one of the scariest things any person could go through with great strength and composure. The pressure of the job was relentless, and she continued to take it on. It didn't take long to realize that the momentum of our company was not going to stop anytime soon.

While my schedule was as full as anyone's, I wanted to do something to take some of the pressure off of Linda. I began to ask her for some additional responsibilities. It was like pulling teeth, but eventually she gave up some of her duties. I started by taking over the travel department, then asset insurance, and eventually assumed some of the office management responsibilities. Linda took several weeks off after her surgery, and while she was going through therapy,

I did my best to hold down the fort. Our profits were starting to rise at a dramatic rate, and it was time to move back into the big leagues, so we brought in an executive who had helped us get through our early heyday.

Steve was a no-nonsense businessman with an accounting and legal background. As soon as he came in, the organization felt the effects of his style of management. Steve and Robert made a pretty good team; Robert could continue to focus on the human side of the business while Steve's attention was on the numbers. In just three short years, the company had grown from barely $4 million to $20 million.

Linda came back to work—wig and all, since the radiation treatment had taken most of her hair. She was strictly focused on human resources, but her stay would be short-lived. She really wanted to do something with her life beyond work and the family. She wanted to be more involved with her church, volunteer work, and helping others. This was something that I knew she would be excellent at. She was such a caring and faith-filled person. I was a better person and a better manager for having worked with her. Before she left, she made sure I would be involved in a project that would solidify my place with ActionSystems.

Linda would eventually go on to become the director at Interfaith Housing Coalition. What an awesome nonprofit organization that helps homeless families get back on their feet, a faith-based program that provides housing, childcare, and counseling in areas like finance, employment, and life skills. Eventually, I would volunteer and because of my background, I could definitely relate.

Back at ActionSystems, my attention had been focused on my many jobs including managing production, purchasing, the in-house print shop, shipping/receiving, office management, travel, asset insurance, and facilities, so I had my hands pretty full. One day, Steve called Linda and me into his office. Steve told us that the majority of the managers were fed up with administrative support. Steve said that he was at the point to just let them all go, not because they weren't good at what they do, it was that they weren't being utilized properly (remember, Steve wasn't a people person). Instead, Linda and I convinced him to let us have a stab at improving the situation. The first thing we did was meet with the administrative assistants to get their side of the story. We discovered that they felt they were doing a great job. From their perspective, they were overworked, underappreciated, and underpaid. From the manager's perspective, they were not getting their money's worth, and they felt the productivity of the assistants was at an all-time low.

> This was a classic example of poor communication. I had already been through this school—the hard way.

After a week of meetings, research, and analysis, we were prepared to meet with Steve. The recommendation was that all of the assistants should report to one manager and receive timely performance feedback. The assistants were not voicing their concerns either. They wanted fair treatment, a balanced workload, support, and the tools to make them and the company successful. I fully expected that Linda would be that manager, and was surprised when Linda and Steve asked me to take on this responsibility. Of course I accepted. It would not be easy, the managers were not crazy about having their assistant supporting them but reporting to someone else. The assistants were upset because I provided them with some very candid feedback on their performance from the managers' view. Still, I was committed to making this work. Despite some criticism of my involvement on both sides, eventually they saw the process working. Our administrative support was getting back on track.

It wasn't long after the success of the administrative reporting structure that Steve thanked me for my commitment and dedication and rewarded me with a promotion to vice president of operations. Along with the title came an increase in salary, a larger bonus percentage, and a generous amount of stock options. I was absolutely elated. I could not believe in less than ten years with the company, I had moved from a box packer in a small warehouse to the vice president of operations for a multi-million-dollar consulting firm. I now had nearly twenty people reporting to me and was responsible for many areas of the company. I was empowered to structure my organization the way I thought it should be done. Since I was finally in a decision-making position, I promoted some of my team to decrease my direct span of control. This way, I could provide better communication and vision. Meanwhile, the organization was growing like wildfire, and the company was changing almost every other day.

It Only Gets Better

My home life was changing as well. Lisa was now pregnant with our first child. Just when I thought I couldn't be anymore excited about life, it just kept getting better. I knew there were forces at play that were greater than me. I had changed my life completely, and I was truly blessed.

We had a beautiful baby girl. She had the largest, most beautiful eyes, and a smile that always stopped me in my tracks. It was as if God was giving me a second chance at raising a daughter, and I was determined to try and be the best father there ever was. Sierra was the joy of my life, and I thought life just couldn't get any better. Every day, I worked hard and couldn't wait to get home to my family. I didn't want to miss one of Sierra's smiles. As I spent more time with Sierra, I'd start to think about the child I had left behind. I decided I wanted to do a better job of being there when Amber needed a dad. I wanted to be more involved in her life.

Amber Alert

I made a real effort to call and talk to Amber more, but it wasn't easy for either of us. She was now a teenager and was really struggling with her emotions. Her insecurities were apparent, and she was already dealing with bouts of depression and uncertainty about her life. I needed to see her, and Lisa was very supportive. So when

Sierra got a little older, we planned a trip for Lisa and Linda to finally meet.

It had been difficult over the past fifteen years for Amber and me to establish a relationship. In the beginning, as soon as we would start to communicate with some regularity, Linda would start calling at two or three in the morning to harass me. She'd be so drunk that I could barely understand her, but she would do her best to make her point. Her points? I didn't spend enough time with Amber; I didn't pay enough child support, that I wasn't living near Amber; I didn't call or write enough and that she (Linda) still loved me. Eventually, my calls to Amber became even less frequent, because I dreaded the thought of having Linda pick up the phone.

So as the years passed, Amber and I became more and more estranged. When we did talk over the phone, we didn't know what to say to each other. Still, every year I would go see her and spend a few days hanging out with her. As she got older, her resentment of me became more obvious, and her relationship with her mother got stranger and stranger. I guess Amber never really knew my side of the story.

One Thanksgiving, Lisa and I took Sierra to visit Amber in Missouri (Linda and Amber moved to a small town in southern Missouri because after five years of not working, Linda finally had a job working at a prison).

We met Jessica (Linda's older daughter) in St. Louis and drove to Linda's apartment about two hours away. Linda and Amber knew we were coming and what time we would be there. When we arrived, no one answered the door, so Jessica turned the doorknob, and the apartment was open. We walked into the small apartment, and it was absolutely trashed. It looked like it had not been cleaned for weeks. As Lisa and I looked at the place in amazement, we were shocked to see a twenty-year-old walking out of Linda's room. The guy had long matted hair, a goatee starting under his chin, dirty jeans, and no shirt. He walked by us, trying not to look us in the eyes so we wouldn't notice how incredibly hung over he was. We asked him if he knew where Linda and Amber were, but he didn't have a clue. I don't think he even knew what day it was.

After an uncomfortable silence, the young man went back into the bedroom, got more clothes on, and left the apartment.

Jessica was visibly embarrassed as she gave us the rest of the tour. The kitchen was filled with dirty dishes and trash; there was partially eaten food on the counter that had obviously been there for days. The bedrooms were just as trashed. The rooms contained nothing but broken-down beds and dressers. Amber had pictures posted all over her walls as her wallpaper. She did her best to give the room that feminine feel with old pink, lacy bed coverings. The shock continued to overwhelm us as we looked at her floor that was littered with all kinds of stuff, including empty beer cans and bottles. Oh my God, did this take me back to a bad place I knew some twenty years ago. I was sick.

After about thirty minutes of waiting, we were about ready to give up when the door suddenly swung open. Linda and Amber had gone shopping at Wal-Mart. They never explained why they weren't there when we arrived or who the young guy was. We immediately noticed that the relationship between Linda and Amber was not a typical mother/daughter relationship but was more like sisters. Now, I don't have a problem with a mother and daughter acting like sisters, but these two were acting like girls that were out of control. Linda was the bad sister, and Amber was trying to be the good one. The rest of the visit was very uncomfortable, to say the least. We took Amber with us to St. Louis and spent a few more uncomfortable days together, and then we returned to Texas.

All the way back and for some time after, I could not get it out of my head what a mistake I had made. I gave up, and because I did Amber's chances of a normal life were slim. It's a thought that to this day haunts me.

That trip was also a snapshot of what my life would have continued to be if I hadn't made choices to change my fate.

Returning to my family life quickly filled my days, and I didn't feel like I had a minute to spare. ActionSystems was now a $30 million dollar company. It had grown from seventeen people to 125. I was now earning a six-figure income, I had been given more stock, and my bills were paid. Lisa no longer had to work and could afford to stay home and raise children. She ended up working part-time so she didn't go brain dead. I stopped working an insane number of hours and couldn't wait to get home to Lisa and Sierra.

I began to realize that my life was becoming balanced. I had time with my family, I had time to exercise, I was getting everything done on the job, and as a family, we were going to church. My faith had been steadily growing, although I didn't really realize what was happening. One day, I found myself looking in the mirror and asking God, "Why did you allow all of these good things to happen to *me*? After all the times I cursed your name, you never turned your back on me. Instead you gave me the strength and ability to survive. You gave me a second, third, fourth (I lose track) chance. Why? What did I do to deserve this great life?"

> I was staring at my reflection and there I was looking right back at me. I realized that God wanted me to serve as an example for others—my life was my testimonial.

Everything I had experienced led me to this point in time—to this realization. I have to do whatever I can to help others who are struggling with some of the same challenges that life had presented to me. It's time to give back. I had finally discovered my purpose. Really, my life had only just begun. Now, how do I do this?

One of the first things I did after this realization was to make a firm attempt to forgive some of the most cruel and devastating things in my past. To put these demons behind me, I decided to write a letter to my dad and Peggy. It took me several tries to write the card asking them to forgive me for all the pain I might have caused them over the years. I was emotionally drained after doing this, but I also felt lighter and relieved of some of the baggage I had been carrying all of these years. With some apprehension, I mailed the card. No response came back. I understood and still forgave. I did what I had to do, and after the many years of the abuse haunting me, I could now let go and the pain and guilt was gone. Still, I felt compelled to give back and to reach out to others. I wasn't sure how to proceed.

I started to share my story with others because I wanted to help people who might have a troubled past as well. One of the first people I shared my story with was Linda Hall. It was a few days before Easter when I sat her down and told her about my past and how much I appreciated what she and Robert had done for me. I asked for her help again, I wanted to find out how I could share my testimonial with others in a way that might benefit those in trouble.

On Easter Sunday, Linda called and apologized for interrupting my family time. She wanted to get me on the phone with Robert's sister, Joan. Joan was a neuropsychologist who specialized in addictions. She was putting together a three-day workshop for a prison farm in Illinois. Her team consisted of her, the clinical expert, and a financial advisor who also happened to be a preacher and a businessman who also helped to finance the workshop. However, Joan was missing one piece to the puzzle of her workshop. She needed someone who could relate to the prisoners. Linda thought that I might be the missing piece.

After Joan and I talked for a while, she was convinced that the Lord had brought us together and we were meant do this workshop together. She told me the only thing that could make this even more perfect was if I was black. Well, I couldn't help her out there, but I gave her confidence that I would be able to relate.

A few months later, the team met in St. Louis and started our journey into a very secluded part of Illinois. Meeting in St. Louis itself was kind of ironic, as that is where my life experienced its greatest challenges. We drove deep into the country to a farm. It was late and pitch dark, but the light of a church led us to the entrance of the church. Inside, we met some of the members. Even though the church was still under construction, it looked great. It was modern looking with plenty of room. As I walked through the corridors, plastic poly was up as a temporary fixture until the doors arrived. Just as I reached to pull one of the plastic doors, it flung open. I about had the pants scared off me from the surprise. A tall black man, as tall as or taller than me (and I'm six-foot-four), came through the poly and grabbed me around my neck and gave me a big hug. Then he stepped back to introduce himself as Pastor Bob Weeden. Immediately, I could tell Pastor Bob wasn't your average run-of-the-mill country preacher. Pastor Bob was dressed in boots, blue jeans, a very colorful shirt, and a straw hat. As I gathered my bearings from the surprise, I looked closely at Pastor Bob. I don't think I have ever seen eyes that looked as intense and committed as his.

It was late, so after the introductions we were assigned to our quarters. Our quarters were old trailers with no heat or air. Since it was the middle of the summer, I wasn't worried about the heat because it was almost 100 degrees even at night. My bed was a bit small, since my feet hung off the end. As I tried to go to sleep, the heat got to be unbearable. I noticed that the windows were covered in plastic, so I tried to pull the plastic back to let some air through. I quickly discovered why the plastic was there. As I lay there with no blankets, I could feel bugs of every variety landing on my body. The light right outside the window acted as a magnet for every flying thing for miles around. Somehow I managed to get some sleep— despite the bugs and my excitement.

Even though I was there in an administrative support role, I was just glad to be there and hoped to make a difference. Joan explained that she wanted me to be behind the scenes and try to bond with some of the participants and act as a conduit between the very different backgrounds that Joan and the guests of the prison farm had. The workshop kicked off with Joan and the team doing a fantastic job to engage most of the group. Some of them seemed to be distant and trying to avoid engaging. During the break, I walked around and met some of the participants. I found that they had a variety of reasons for going through the prison farm, which wasn't really a prison. It was more like a halfway house before they were released back into society. Many were there for drug abuse, some were there for burglary, some for robbery and a myriad of other crimes.

I'll never forget trying to introduce myself to one of the guys who was gathered with his "posse." His name was Darryl and he had taken the attitude that he didn't know why we were there. He said, "You guys aren't going to tell me anything that I don't already know." He went on to say that he had a degree, was a schoolteacher, managed, and even owned his own business. Darryl continued to take the attitude that he was going to resist any coaching that we were going to provide. As long as Darryl resisted the coaching, so would his followers. Apparently there was one thing Darryl didn't resist—crack cocaine, which is what cost Darryl his careers.

The next two days of the workshop went really well as Joan did a great job sharing exercises to help these twenty-six guys learn how to go back into a relationship and be in touch with and in control of their emotions. They also learned how to do basic financial planning and how to get started at a job, no matter what level they start at.

I played my role behind the scenes and was doing really well with the guys. In the meantime, I kept a watchful eye on Darryl. I could see him in the back of the room falling asleep and when he was awake, you could see he was not paying attention. Some of the exercises included breakout sessions where we got into groups and shared some of the mistakes that got us to where we were today. I shared my stories and many were surprised that I was not as squeaky clean as they expected me to be.

On the night before the last day of the workshop, I could not sleep all night. I tossed and turned, and I know to some of you this is going to sound strange, but I was hearing voices in my head. They were telling me to "let go" and that I needed to "open up." The voice told me that my purpose is to help these people and to serve as an example. I could not sit back without sharing the testimonial of why I was where I was, and why I am who I am. It was time for the "The Purpose."

The next morning, I shot out of the trailer and left to meet Joan. As I caught up with her at the church, she was frantically preparing for the last day of the workshop. I walked into the room and was quickly thrown into the rush of helping to get ready. In the middle of the rush, I just stopped and asked Joan if I could share something with her, she stopped to listen. I first apologized because I knew that my role was just to be her assistant and do whatever I was asked, but I felt I had to take a new role. I shared my story and what happened to me last night. Thinking that she might be upset, I prepared for her reasons why that couldn't happen. Instead, tears filled her eyes and she said, "Hallelujah, praise the Lord!"

Joan immediately changed the format; instead of a classroom-style format, she put the group in a large circle. In the middle of the circle, she put two chairs. That is where Joan and I sat. She began to ask me a series of questions and every dark secret I ever had was brought to the surface. My soul felt like it was getting cleansed in front of a captive audience (literally). Here I was supposed to be some kind of tough guy relating to other tough guys, and I was sharing a past of being sexually abused, physically abused, my break-downs, and near suicides. I told the stories of how my stepmom, stepbrothers, real mom, and others had abused me for years, how I was a drug addict to almost every type of drug mentionable.

I described how alcohol was a daily routine in my life. How I had been homeless and I had to crawl from the very bottom of the streets to get back to even be a productive contributor in society, then had to work even harder to become successful. When it was all over, it was as if I was sharing the truth with myself and not with a room full of strangers. After Joan asked her last question, I cautiously looked around the room to see the response. The majority of the audience was in tears. Then the strangest thing occurred. The inmates started sharing their testimonials of abuse in their childhood and teenage years. The most amazing thing was that one by one, these tough guys were walking up to me and hugging me. For that moment, I wasn't white and they weren't black. It wasn't about the "haves" and the "have-nots"; we were just people who had shared some of the same pain.

I felt a huge hand rest upon my shoulder. As I turned, it was Darryl with tears running down his face. We embraced, and I could feel his tears on my shoulder as he told me in my ear what had happened to him. Darryl was only eight years old when he heard a noise in his sister's bedroom. Darryl entered his sister's room to find her being assaulted by his mom's boyfriend. Darryl tried to stop the man, but he was overpowered and Darryl was sexually violated by the man. He has spent all the following years trying to be the tough guy because he wasn't big enough or bad enough at the time to help his little sister. He had never shared that story with anyone until that day. And on that day, Darryl, I, and I am sure others were freed from the past. This experience was just another affirmation of my purpose for being.

Chapter 17:

Having A Purpose Is Hard Work

So there I was, a vice president of a growing consulting firm and after all it took to get me here, I was still under forty. Things were going very well for me in all areas. I was surrounded by good people with good values. I would go on to become a senior vice president of operations. The company that Robert built became one of the best small businesses to work for in Dallas. I was giving it my all at work and at home. I knew what I wanted to do to give back, but was still struggling to find the right outlet. Work intervened while this calling continued to take shape inside me.

In 1998, ActionSystems was in need of a spark in the e-commerce arena. Customer Analytics (CA) was a Massachusetts-based company dedicated to making its name in the booming dot-com industry. They had a solid product and happy customers. CA would be just the catalyst ASI needed to catapult our success through the Internet.

.Com or .Bomb?

Robert and the President of CA made a big splash to announce the "merger." We rented out a theater in the Galleria Mall in Dallas, and the two company leaders did a big presentation about how great this merger would be for everyone.

This company we acquired turned out to be a group of hardworking employees who were dedicated to achieving a cash-out option. CA was the prime example of the dot-com explosion. Venture capitalists were throwing money into any company that said they were a dot-com software provider. This company knew all they had to do was get their name out there, and they would be millionaires. Customer Analytics' nearly fifteen employees came into ASI and piled up more expenses than all of our 100-plus employees. Instead of strong software, their product turned out to be "vaporware" and their customers were angry and up in arms that they had been waiting for a reliable product that was yet to be delivered.

The result was a drain on the company so massive that we could not recover. I am sure ASI management had the dot-com bug and saw a way to cash-out as well. After only two years, we were challenged just to meet payroll. We were all working very hard and really wanted to achieve our goals, but we were in too deep.

In April of 2000, all the employees were called together, and Robert announced that we were the product of an acquisition. Once again, management tried to spin this as exciting news. We were being acquired by an international company of over 500 employees. It was a public company whose stock in January of 2000 was trading at over $100 a share. I had over 30,000 shares, so it sounded like it could be a good thing. I tried to be positive. But my positive attitude soon turned to pain as I spent the next two days laying off those employees who helped our company to be successful for years. The office was filled with tears, anger, and shock. No one knew who was next. How can something that was presented as such a positive thing feel so wrong? Now what was I going to do?

I was soon to be back at square one—and this time, it wasn't only me who would be in jeopardy.

My wife and I had just completed our family with the birth of our baby boy. As fate would have it, on my last shot (no pun intended), along came Brayden. I was really excited because between my brother and me we had five girls but no boys. But how would I be able to take care of my family without a job?

I guess once again He was looking out for me, because I was spared and instead of a pink slip, I was presented with an offer letter to work for the new company, Exchange Applications, Inc. I decided to accept this offer, but the changes would continue. For the next two years, I was a director of global operations. I took my "real" trip overseas to London to help set up an operation. But it was just a matter of time before it would end. The market in the new millennium is merciless for a publicly traded software company who missed its number like we did for two consecutive quarters. Our fate was sealed. The dot-com companies were falling one after another, and we fell into that category. In October of 2000, just nine short months after Exchange took over, that stock, which had traded for $100 a share, had plummeted to eighteen cents a share. It was a "fire sale" at Exchange. The first round of layoffs came, and then the next round. Eventually the office in Dallas looked like an empty shell of its former self.

The last day of the office came in September of 2001. Everyone was gone, and I was coordinating an auction to sell everything I could so Exchange could stay in business up in Boston. The auction went well, and I sent in more than a hundred thousand dollars to Boston. As I was standing alone in the empty office, then walking the halls shutting off the lights for the last time, I recalled the thirteen years and all the good times and the great appreciation I had for all of the employees. They probably would never realize how they touched my life and changed me forever. Now standing in the dark and open area, I could see the Dallas skyline shimmering as if to say, there is still a light of hope burning out there. Which one will be yours?

Before my last day, I was contacted by the former CFO at Exchange who heard I was leaving. I was surprised because I had butted heads with George more than any other executive at Exchange. We had deep fundamental differences on how to treat vendors and employees. For example, I thought employee's expenses and vendors should be paid for work and services delivered. George had other uses for that money that he thought was keeping us in business.

I had been holding out hope at Exchange that I would receive a similar severance package as the first round of layoffs, since I stuck around as the "last man standing." In terms of years of service and seniority, I had been there from ASI to CA to Exchange for thirteen years, and two weeks of severance for every year was significant. I would not have to work for seven months. With this package, I could start my own business, like I had always wanted. Alas, my dream would be put on hold, as I found out I would only receive one week of severance for every year of service. This meant I would need a job soon and would be job hunting during the holidays.

They say business makes strange bedfellows. Well, that held true, since George wanted me to come to work with him at his new company, ChartOne. He recruited me harder than I have ever been recruited to come over to his company. It wasn't an easy decision. After the reduced severance, George's offer suddenly got more intriguing. I accepted. I turned off the lights to ASI/CA/Exchange on a Friday evening at 7:30 p.m. and boarded a plane at 5:00 a.m. that following Monday on my way to the ChartOne corporate in sunny California, where a whole new adventure would begin. I wasn't sure how this would fit in with my purpose to give back, but I had to trust and follow the road I was on.

Chapter 18:

↑

Charting a New Course

ChartOne was a medical records management company that had been in business for over twenty years, with more than 1,200 employees in forty-six states. In 2000, they were spun off from a large, publicly traded company called Quadramed to create its own entity focusing on the future of electronic medical records (EMR). They had been a low-profit, high-volume business for years, so saving money anywhere would only benefit the bottom line.

The ChartOne headquarters was located right across the street from the San Jose airport. George was not able to meet me in San Jose—in fact it would be four months before I would see him face to face. Except for some brief phone interviews, I walked into the office not knowing anyone. It didn't take long before I became engaged with my new company and its challenges.

For the next four plus years, I was involved in all aspects of the company. I managed all areas of purchasing, distribution, facilities, shipping, and travel management. My job? Save money and improve service. And that's what my team did. During those four years, the company saved millions through vendor re-negotiations, new policies, cost consolidation, cross-training employees, and other efficiencies. I was putting my experience and learning to work for ChartOne. I worked to get to know my employees and do right by them to earn their trust and respect.

I was also asked to look into selling a business unit that was losing money. The storage business for ChartOne was losing tens of thousands every year, and ChartOne didn't want to deal with it anymore. I reviewed the business and conducted an analysis. The company executives were surprised at my findings. I recommended we stay in this business! This business had potential, and our customers valued this service from ChartOne. If we sold it, we would risk millions in lost core services revenue. I suggested that we assign a manager who would take the time to focus on the business. We could make money in this business. The executives came back and said, "Good work. Okay, that manager is *you*. Go for it!"

You Da Man

Wait a second! I've never run a business unit before, nor have I been in sales or marketing. I haven't interacted with external customers. Still, they turned the business over to me with the caveat that I had one year, and if the business was not profitable, they would shut it down.

In the next year, I learned so much more than I could have in any classroom about running a business. I had to.

> I dove in headfirst and became addicted to learning all I could about this part of the business, the customers, our products, and our services.

I realized that customers didn't want to talk to a salesperson—they wanted someone who could save them money and provide good service. Hey, that is what I have been doing throughout my fledgling career. I created marketing campaigns, did sales presentations, met with customers, and listened. I was presenting to senior financial decision makers for large healthcare systems. This was a long way from the guy that hid behind the curtain, hoping he would not be called on in an employee meeting. The business started to grow. The first year the business broke even and for the next three years, the annual business revenue and profits grew from a half million dollars a year in revenue that was losing 20 percent, to over $2 million in revenue with a 20 percent profit. Not bad for a guy who didn't have a clue what he was doing and was doing it part-time. During this period, I still had my *real* job managing the other areas of ChartOne. I could only devote about 20 percent of my time to the records management division.

In 2004, in another cost management initiative, we relocated our administration offices from San Jose to my hometown in Dallas. This changed my job once again. I was to set up this office and be the senior manager. George also placed our collections and customer service teams under my tutelage and development. To say I was spread thin would be an understatement. I learned as much from staff as they could have ever learned from me. And I grew.

Pissed Off with Politics

I'm not sure I will ever understand executive politics. What I do know is that it's everywhere! I had never been one that fit into an "executive" mold; I was always on the outside of executive teams, and I was okay with that. The challenges would be handed to me, and I would deliver. Many times, others got the promotions and took the credit. I didn't mind because it just seemed to work out. George had spent the last three years of my reviews telling me he was preparing me for that "next level" and each year there was an "if you can do this" promise. Each year, I achieved the "ifs." He talked about the next level being a VP of Administration, but we just weren't big enough yet.

Heading into my review in 2005, I fully expected to get a new set of "ifs" since I completed the old ones. I was okay with this, because I enjoyed the challenge and the learning. I received a great review. So you can probably imagine the look on my face during the review when George said, "You've done a *great* job with all your responsibilities!" And in the next breath, "I'm going to promote our attorney, have him come to Dallas, and you will report to him." In other words, "gift wrap" your accomplishments because they will become our VP of Administration's success stories.

I was devastated and furious! How can this be? Our attorney had no experience in any of these areas, and he had only managed two people in his career. I had sixty-two people reporting to me. This made no sense. I was blown away and confused. George was not able to provide any good explanation. I chalked it up to politics. I had to accept it and be thankful that I had a job. I had to continue to trust that someone had a plan for me that I could not understand at the moment.

For days and nights after that, I relived the conversation and wracked my brain trying to come up with what I could have done wrong. I got a great review, I got a great raise, but someone else got the job. Tell me that's not mixed signals! I searched my soul, I stressed, and I lost my will, my energy, and my passion. I was hurting inside constantly, and I didn't know what I was going to do, but I couldn't take this feeling. I had never even thought about looking for another job. I didn't have a clue where to start looking for a job in a position like I had for the past eighteen years.

A Call to My Voice of Reason

I needed some advice and guidance, so I talked to my wife, my friends, and some former colleagues. Most of the feedback was divided; one side made the point that they're paying you a great salary, you should feel lucky and not ruin your career (meaning a career I probably shouldn't have had in the first place). The other side was upset, thought it was unfair, and felt I should look for another job. Then I made that call to the one person that I could always depend on for the right answer. Former CEO and now semi-retired Robert Hall listened intently as he always did. When I was exhausted from venting and took a breath he said, "Mike, you know I have always seen you as an entrepreneur. I have always known that one day you would run your own business. Look at what you have done for ChartOne's records management business."

It was like of bolt of lightning raced through my body.

The force hit me and suddenly life and energy started to surge in my body. The fear that has always driven me was back; the risk that has always led to success was back.

Robert's few words of faith and belief in me gave me the unstoppable energy to go for it. I was excited and ready, but I also knew that there was much work to be done and much to learn. I knew what I had to do, and how it would fit into my purpose.

During the middle of ChartOne's national meeting, I scheduled a private meeting with the CEO, the CFO, and our general counsel. After I vented a bit, I am sure the three of them thought I was going to turn in my notice. So you could feel the pause in the room when I made the statement, "I would like to buy the storage (records management) business from ChartOne."

After a few minutes of making sure I was serious and trying to help me realize what a big decision this was, they asked, "What happens if this doesn't work out?"

I told them that I did not want focus on what may not happen; instead, I wanted to understand what I needed to do to make it happen. They agreed that if I made a legitimate offer, they would put the offer before the Board for approval.

An offer was made, and eventually it was accepted. There was only one problem: I didn't have a clue where I was going to come up with the over $1 million it was going to take to buy this business. Over the next four months, I went through an intense process of trying to raise the funding. I tried various options to finance this deal. I had some good support, but I just couldn't line up the minimum number of investors with the money to make it work. I met with bank after bank, I filled out forms and more forms, I made presentation after presentation, and I got really close. While my credit was great, there were not enough tangible assets to give the bank a comfort level that they had something to repossess.

Then I was introduced to a group of VCs (Venture Capitalists). I presented my case and made my presentation, and they got it! They knew the potential, they understood the direction, and they saw the exit strategy. But what they really saw was how they would line up the funding. I would do all the work, and they would make a major profit from their relatively small investment.

So I had my investors. I had the backing of the VC's CFO, legal services. I had accounting help. I had everything that I needed to run the operation, and even though it would come with a heavy price, it would be worth it. The due diligence process had begun; we were finally going to know if the business was worth all I thought it would be. Then we discovered that there was a loan on the books that belonged to ChartOne that they wanted us to pick up. They were insistent that it needed to be part of the deal. We agreed to pay it if we could reduce the amount of the offer accordingly. And it was at that point that the dream of owning a business fell apart.

In addition to the loan issue, in the past several months, I had been focusing on my other duties at ChartOne, along with spending every spare minute working on funding for the purchase. As a result, the storage business took a hit and the business's revenue was down with no significant new accounts in sight. This caused my investors to become nervous. They adjusted the offer price down to $0, but we would assume all the assets and liabilities. This would never fly with the ChartOne CFO, and he said as much.

After the deal fell apart, I was back to the point of confusion, disappointment, and at a loss about my future. I felt it was only a matter of time before ChartOne would replace me. They knew my disappointment and they did not have any challenges to match that of running my own company. And looking back, why would they want to sell the business to me when basically they "had their cake and were able to eat it too"? They had me doing several jobs for them, including running and building the storage services division. If I left and took the storage business with me, who would take care of all the other departments that were my responsibility? But neither ChartOne nor I was prepared for what happened next.

Chapter 19:

When a Door Closes,
a Window Opens

At the time, very few people knew about my intent to buy the ChartOne storage business. One of the people who did was our general counsel, Joe. This person also happened to be my successor, who was promoted into the position I had been previously working for years to earn.

In the latter stages of my hunt for funding to buy the ChartOne storage business, Joe approached me about a call he received. The call was from someone he knew in the Northeast who was in contact with a company that was looking for someone to run their company. Joe passed the contact information along to me. I had put it out of my mind for a few weeks while I focused on the purchase initiative at hand. Eventually, I made the call, and a new door opened. Over the next few weeks, I went back and forth with my main contact, John, their contract CFO. I spent a lot of time trying to understand the company and reviewing documents and financials.

Initially, I had turned down the offer and let John know. He said that it was unfortunate, since he felt that I was a good match for the business. I thanked him and let him know if I could be any help to give me a call. This simple little closing courtesy offer turned to a conversation that spanned the next couple of months. We finally met face-to-face at their location in Providence, Rhode Island. There I met the owner and John. During an eight-hour period, they shared their business model, history, and desire to build an attractive company for possible partners. I shared my background, history, and what brought me to the point of calling them.

The owner, Tom, shared that he was ready to retire, and he would like to build the business and use the funds as his retirement. However, the business was falling on tough times because they had just lost one of their largest customers, and they were in the middle of litigation that made possible suitors shy away from the purchase. During our day together, I got the feeling that I had not felt in almost twenty years. It was the same feeling I had when I stepped through the doors of ActionSystems, "There is something about this company." The three of us seemed to hit it off well. At the end of the day, we left "the door open" for future discussions and I headed back to Dallas.

Trust Turns the Tide

Then came the offer. It included an exit strategy for Tom and a significant opportunity for me to head up a company as a CEO. It also included an option to buy the company, and I would share in the proceeds with Tom. They were so trusting that after one face-to-face visit, Tom was willing to put his seventy-five-year-old, family-owned business into my hands. I was floored, but realized that this was meant to be.

There was not a lot of surprise at ChartOne when I turned in my resignation, but the look on George's face when I said I was leaving to become the CEO of a company was priceless. George had told me that CEO was his dream job. He had said that my education and the fact that I did not have an advanced degree had been holding me back. Yet, here I was, CEO of the Quinlan Companies. Imagine that.

This story brings me to the present. At this point, I do not know if I will be able to take this company to the expected success. I do know I will work as hard as I can to try to get the company there—I

MICHAEL G. COOLEY

will give it my all. So far, our revenues have doubled. And to show that everything comes back to you, the Quinlan Companies acquired the three divisions that I was responsible for at ChartOne. Again I say, "Imagine that!"

Now in a position where I have an opportunity to influence so many people, I view every relationship as a special gift. I work hard to make interactions a positive experience. I learn so much from every story that each person has to share. I learn and grow every day and I put everything I have into my family, my job, my spirituality, myself, and especially my purpose. I hope to make a positive difference in as many lives as possible through work and through other avenues.

What's Next?

Well, it's time to pay back all that I have been given in my life. I am in a place in my life where I can do just that! I hope to make up for all that I have done wrong and all the people I have hurt along the way. One of the ways that I feel I can give back and help others is to share my life's story. I decided to do this in hopes it touches and helps people who might be living a troubled life like I did. I want them to know that there are others who understand what they are going thru.

> I can meet people where they are and can relate completely to the anger, fear, frustration, and feeling of being utterly lost. I've been there many times. My message is this: if I can change the course of my life, so can you.

My dream is to be able to spend my life helping others on both sides of the fence. This includes those who are lost, desolate, without hope, and without a roof over their heads at night, as well as those leaders who have everything yet are still lost and empty. If the empty people with the means could find a way to reach out and help others in need, they too would have purpose. Just being a mentor or showing that people can care unconditionally would do so much to raise up those who are lost and in need. It's those individuals that fall down along the way and because there is no one to help them get up they stay down. Having someone to care and guide them will do so much to inspire hope and help them reach their potential. Together we can all achieve our potential and fulfill our purposes for being here.

To anyone who is struggling with addictions, hopelessness, physical or mental abuse, please don't stop trying to achieve your dreams! Don't give up! Besides my own story, there are many testimonials of people who have had it much worse than I did and still achieved their dreams and found their purpose. I know you can do it! Find someone to reach out to, or call me! When you find someone to help and believe in you, you understand how blessed you truly are. Then it's your turn: Live your life with purpose, and help someone else get up and find their wings so they can soar. There is no greater success than that.

Who knows exactly how my story will end? I'm just living those chapters now. I'll get back to you on that!

Looking Back

After everything, after all was said and done in my climb back into society, I realized that I had to 'unlearn' so many things about how I was raised that had misguided my past. However, in return for all that open space in my head, I learned so many new things about life. I learned how important it is to always be on the lookout for new opportunities. I realized that all that is ever expected of you is your very best. If you are trying to break bad habits and make better choices, you have to surround yourself with the right people. Mentors and role models were absolutely critical to my rebound. Then there are those very special people you meet along the way that love you unconditionally and want you to be successful, but if at first you don't succeed, they are right there by your side because they know you will not give up. With this new path, these new people, and this new education, I feel equipped to actually help those in my past and those I have yet to meet who are heading down the wrong path. Maybe I am not an expert, but I am in fact a living example of someone who survived and thrived where many have given up.

Epilogue

Where Are They Now?

Many nights as I was working late, I would walk the halls of the of the office tower turning out the lights on the floor. I would stop and gaze at the lit up skyline of downtown Dallas. I almost have to pinch myself because it's hard to believe how blessed I am. I feel I have everything that I could ever want. I think about those I've known throughout the tough times in my life and wonder where they are. A number of those in my past died premature deaths from alcoholism, drugs, or some form of violence. I am truly blessed not to be one of them.

The old gang: From time to time, I go back to Gainesville to visit my family or go to St. Louis and visit my brother. In St. Louis, my brother and I visited some of the old haunts (neighborhood bars) that my mom made her second home. One evening, we walked into the bar that held the List. (The list contained names of people that were banned from the bar for various reasons such as fighting, drunkenness, bad credit, etc.) The list had been updated from the old days—most of them are dead. Now the list is a collection of some of the kids I used to run with as a teenager. Going into the place was like stepping back in time. We saw many from the old gang and our troubled days. They were the same—drunk, some were unemployed, unshaven, wearing tattered clothes. They looked and smelled like they hadn't bathed for days. Yet they were different—older, run-down looking with gray hair and missing teeth. It was obvious that the constant drugs and alcohol had gotten the best of them.

You could see the surprise when they recognized who I was. The last time they had seen me I was at my worst state, just before I disappeared. I couldn't tell you the number of people that walked up to me and said, "Cooley, I thought you were dead." One of the guys we used to hang out with as kids was Bernice. He was bragging about being forty and just having his first heart attack. A month after visiting the bar, that same guy had his second heart attack but wasn't around to brag about it because it killed him.

We also ran into some of our old running buddies in Gainesville. We even ran into Larry, (the popular, cool drug dealer from Hawaii). We found him living in the back of an old commercial warehouse, sleeping on a dirty blanket in a bed of dirt. He had nothing; he was filthy and slurring to the point of being incoherent. Another wasted soul lost to drugs and alcohol.

Marty: My only real brother is another example of someone who survived. He has raised a wonderful family. Married a couple of years before me, he now has three grown girls, two of whom he adopted. He still runs the car dealerships in St. Louis and has become quite the fledgling real estate mogul. He is buying properties and using his carpentry skills to fix them up and re-sell the houses. We are still really close, and he is also an inspiration to me. He is truly another success story.

Donna: My sister finally had a child after eight miscarriages. Whether it was the problems getting pregnant or her drugs and alcoholism, her son Ty has never been able to walk properly. Donna continued to struggle with drug and alcohol problems. She moved from place to place and couldn't seem to hold down a job. In 2005, I received a call from Ty to let me know that he came home and found his mom dead in her bed. The autopsy showed she had died of a combination of vodka and Valium. My brother and I paid for the funeral. I traveled to St. Louis and delivered the eulogy for my half-sister. Her real brother Ken, the evangelist minister, did send some money to help out with the arrangements, but he never made it to the funeral.

The funeral was surreal. There was Donna laid to rest at the same funeral home as my mom, in the same room at almost the same age as my mom when she died. A lot of people came, and they all had a lot of pleasant things to say about Donna. It is a shame; she could have done so much good. She was so strong yet so weak when it came to drugs and alcohol. She was so much like my mom.

Ken: Because it was at a point that we needed him most, Marty always resented how Ken did not reach out to us after our mom's funeral. I have tried to learn to forgive—life is just too short. Marty grew up admiring Ken, thinking he was the only mentor he could look up to. I guess sometimes it is hard when you learn that everyone is flawed. I know Ken was trying to distance himself from the life he had left. At the time, Ken was also still trying to get his own life together. I can't say that I blame him. Life was tough back then. I continue to communicate with Ken, and occasionally we get together. He has a successful ministry in San Antonio and speaks at churches throughout the country. He has probably saved millions of kids through his ministry. His kids are grown and have lives of their own.

Lionel: My half brother, Lionel, is in a homosexual relationship and it wasn't until my father passed away that he was honest about the relationship. He and his partner have outlasted most relationships and since our dad passed away, he feels he can be honest with himself and be who he is. Today, Lionel and his significant other, Bud, live in Texas and we all have become much closer as a family. Lionel has matured significantly and has had a long career as a corporate sales director in the hotel industry.

David: My stepbrother David is now in his fifties and morbidly overweight. He was a truck driver, but he has chronic back problems, so he no longer works. He lives off the disability he receives for his back. Apparently he lives in constant pain. David lives in a small apartment in Gainesville, and he has no one in his life. David is truly living a lonely existence.

Kenneth: My other stepbrother, Kenneth, went on to marry a stripper and they had three children. Kenneth and Trish continued to drink and do drugs. They were living in Gainesville until his wife left him and moved to Alabama. Ken chased after her and the kids, and eventually the kids came back. Several years ago, I received another call. Ken was drinking with his thirteen-, fourteen-, and seventeen-year-old kids when he fell over dead right in front of them. Cause of death: alcohol poisoning. Kenneth was dead at forty-three and I was a part of another funeral and eulogy. Only a few people showed up to the funeral, including his oldest son, Kenny. Kenny showed up with a group of other kids, looking somewhat stoned and out of it. He showed no emotions throughout the entire funeral. It was kind of ironic that none of the people who were close to him spoke at the funeral, yet my brother and I, whom he abused for years, stood up there, recalling what few good memories we had and said prayers for our abusive stepbrother.

Dad and Peggy: My dad and my stepmother lived in the country outside of Gainesville in an old broken-down trailer house. Dad was proud to say that he just made his last payment on it. Still a few payments to go on the little patch of land the trailer sits on though. Alas, the country was just too far away for Peggy's failing health, so they moved back into town, getting what they could for the trailer. My dad is in his eighties and only recently quit his part-time job. Now living on Social Security and Peggy's disability, they may make less than $22,000 a year. However, they too have their addiction, and it lies in the bingo parlors. Any money they have seems to go to the bingo dealer.

In her seventies, Peggy was bound to a wheel chair. She became so overweight that she started having all types of problems. One problem was that her legs could not support her girth any longer.

She was always at the doctor for treatments, which included draining the fluid from her legs because they would swell. Once, in a restaurant, we had to escort her to the bathroom because her legs just started to bleed and pus was seeping through her skin and bandages. Peggy struggled to do anything for herself, so my dad spent most of his time trying to take care of her. I don't think this is the way he envisioned his dream. Peggy died a few years ago.

Dad was eighty-three when Peggy died. Shortly thereafter, he had to put his dog of twelve years to sleep. His dog was like one of his kids.

It didn't take long after the death of Peggy and Rocky (my dad's dog); my dad was diagnosed with stage four lung cancer. Eighteen years after he quit smoking, it caught up with him; nine months to the day of Peggy's passing, my dad passed away. During his battle with cancer it was the three brothers, Marty, Lionel, and I, who came together and as a family did all we could do to try and save our dad. He was a man who worked hard all his life, was always underappreciated and was never able to achieve his dream, or did he? It's funny; he never really spoke to our face about loving us kids or how proud he was of us and what we had become until the last few years. He was so excited to tell Marty and me about Lionel's success or to tell Lionel and me about Marty's success and so on. I think he truly received some joy seeing how his kids turned out. Not too long before he passed, he told us how proud he was of the way we turned out. Behind the scenes, I hear that he talked about us with pride and maybe he was able to achieve a little bit of his own dreams through our purpose.

I drove or flew the long distance many times to take care of Dad during his last months. I tried to be the strong one and kept my emotions in check. My brothers would break down in tears and anger about my dad's situation, but I always tried to be in control.

Dad was buried at that same little church I used to go to as a kid, the one that Joe Dotson introduced me to way out in the country. The day of the funeral was also surreal. There I was back at that church, but it had grown. They had built a new church next door and who was the pastor? None other than Joe's dad. Seeing Joe's mom and dad again and going through the pictures of Joe was tough enough.

We weren't expecting a big turnout because Peggy and dad didn't have a lot of friends or family near the end. Besides, it was a long drive and the church was hard to find. I felt bad for all the people that did not get to really know who my dad was. Then I walked out the door of the church and saw cars pulling into the parking lot one after another. It was just too much to contain. There were folks that my dad knew, but there were people from ActionSystems and ChartOne who drove for miles to be there. And there was Robert, showing his support. As I delivered the eulogy, I cried. I *cried*. I haven't cried like this since the abuse had hardened me as a child.

Robert: Speaking of Robert, remember I spoke about how when one door closes and a door, window, or something else opens? And you recall how Robert had a business where at one point he was worth $50 million dollars but when Exchange crashed in ten short months, he left his business for a grand total of $0 (*zero*). This was the kind of thing that just should not happen to good people. Well just as that door closed, Robert struck natural gas on some property he had in Oklahoma, which put him in a position to never have to work again. Today he focuses on his church duties, and he has written another book. How can I even begin to describe how influential he is to who I am today?

Lisa, Sierra, and Brayden: My family is a constant beacon that keeps my darkest days behind me in the rearview mirror. My wife is a great mom who manages a fantastic household and family that I am thrilled to be part of. Sierra is growing to be a beautiful, talented young lady, and her witty sense of humor has me laughing all the time. Brayden has become a great all-around athlete that sometimes I am lucky enough to coach. He is also a very caring soul with an incredibly kind heart.

Me: And just who am I? I am a dad, a husband, a brother, a coach, a colleague, and hopefully a mentor. I have reached a point where I can afford to help my extended family financially and developmentally. I try to help them whenever I can, but once again it is a challenge because each has their own circumstances. I hope to use the next phase of my life to help others see that they have a choice and a chance to change their lives. If I can, others can. This book is my life and my therapy from the past. I am a broken man, with many flaws. I have made many bad choices along the way, but I also made just enough right choices to survive and be here today to look in the mirror and say, "Why am I here?" I am here to make a difference. I am here to help others.

I have a purpose and a mission to use my past to make a difference in the future!

Me in Early Elementary

Marty and Me

Lionel, Me, and Marty

Drawing, my Pastime as a Kid

Drawing to Escape

Troubled Teen Years

Mom

Me at the office in the late '80s

Drawing to Relieve Stress

MICHAEL G. COOLEY

Contact Information

Michael Cooley is a business development executive with over twenty years of experience. His career took him from working in the mailroom, with no college education, to being the CEO of a multi-million-dollar company. Mike lives in Coventry, Rhode Island, with his wife, Lisa, and his two children, Sierra and Brayden. To learn more about Michael or to contact him about possible speaking engagements, contact him at mgcooley@gmail.com or visit his website at michaelgcooley.tatepublishing.com.